For Nori, Haruki
and Yukito.

·

And to my mother,
for teaching me
the joy of cooking.

A YEAR OF SIMPLE FAMILY FOOD

Delicious recipes to feed your
family through the seasons

JULIA
BUSUTTIL
NISHIMURA

plum.

Pan Macmillan Australia

CONTENTS

INTRODUCTION

'I ... like food very much, but I never feel like a king or an emperor. I like very simple food: spaghetti with fresh tomato sauce and garlic, green vegetables with good oil and vinegar, rice with very small and sweet peas, maybe asparagus with hard-boiled eggs, if it's the season. I like to eat on a white and clean table near the sea, with friends telling stories and sailing boats travelling far away, up and down.'

•

ETTORE SOTTSASS – ARCHITECT AND DESIGNER

Simple cooking is what I've always known and loved. It is the sort of food I grew up eating – thoughtful, considered and uncomplicated, in the best possible way. If we had good ingredients to begin with, little was needed to make a beautiful meal. This idea was reawakened by my time in the Italian countryside, a place which profoundly impacted the way I cook. I was reminded again years later, this time in Japan, where even the most basic ingredients are cherished, seasons are auspicious and uncomplicated cooking is celebrated.

Food and family are so intertwined. While cooking for family is, of course, to satisfy hunger, it is so much more. 'Family food' is generous and unfussy and demonstrates love and care – it is perfectly imperfect. For me, it is also about making rituals and creating special moments together; even something as simple as eggs on toast can be a joyous occasion when you are all together around the dining table. That notion of being together and sharing food at a table is a practice that is often lost in the busyness of our lives. No matter what the day has brought us, the dependable act of setting the table and enjoying a simple meal is comforting and ever-reassuring.

There is a term in Japanese: *ichi-go ichi-e*. It describes the unrepeatable nature of a moment and, although it specifically refers to traditional tea ceremonies, it can also be used to describe all facets of our lives, including food and cooking. Moments and encounters are always unrepeatable, so it encourages us to find joy in the simple things, knowing that every small moment is just once in a lifetime, never to be experienced again. It prompts me to appreciate the daily meals shared with my family at our table, the centre of our home, or to treasure that first bite of a summer's peach, which will surely not taste the same the following summer, or the following day for that matter.

When apples stretch across the year and potatoes are ever-present, knowing what is in season can be a challenge. Having a guide or a map stuck to your fridge is a practical way to know what is at its prime and when. Even better guides are farmers' markets or greengrocers who really pride themselves in offering only what is in season. Eventually, you will fall into the habit of only choosing what is at its best, rather than automatically reaching for the corn even if it is noticeably expensive and not looking so great. It will make you a more creative and intuitive cook, finding substitutes and broadening your tastes. I never go to the markets with a shopping list – I don't know what will be there, so how can I? Instead, I search for what looks interesting, or perfectly ripe and ready. Only once I'm home do I decide what I will cook.

Having a well-stocked pantry is essential for this to work, too. The fresh and non-perishable items come together in harmony and the idea for a new recipe or a well-loved one will emerge. My time living in Italy taught me that the shopping part is just as important as the cooking. There, no one expects to see the exact same ingredients at the market week to week, so when a particular ingredient is around, it is enjoyed and celebrated because it might not be available next time. There's an emphasis on local, too – perhaps out of pride, but also because it is what makes sense. The bread from a particular bakery, the meat from the butcher, fish from the fishmonger, olive oil direct from the producer, cheese from the sheep farm – shopping for the week's food there was a wonderful experience rather than a chore. While these kinds of rituals are not always possible or geographically feasible to cultivate, the more care you take in selecting ingredients and produce, the more simple – and delicious – the cooking will be.

And while it may seem romantic to talk about shopping in this way, there are many tangible practical reasons to eat with the seasons, namely price, taste and sustainability. Produce that has been grown in season is abundant and therefore much more affordable than something out of season, which is likely to have travelled a long way to get to you or have been grown in a way that requires far more energy and resources. My priorities are seasonality and locality, so these are always at the forefront of my mind when shopping. The overarching motive is that food in season tastes so much better.

There are some recipes in this book that include ingredients that do stretch across seasons. For example, potatoes in summer. Some exceptions are necessary, and ingredients like onions, potatoes and garlic do well stored for months. But there are other ingredients like tomatoes, which I would almost consider an early autumn fruit, or peaches that I don't even bother with out of season. They're either lacking in flavour and/or imported, so they simply don't have a place in my kitchen and I would rather wait. Then there are recipes that may seem like they're not really attached to a season and that is because some of them are not. Certain braises or baked goods, which rely more on pantry supplies, are for the year in its entirety, but I have placed them within the season when I crave them the most or where it sits best with me. There are the fruits or vegetables that barely get a mention – cherries, for example, do not last long enough in our house to be cooked into anything and I usually much prefer eating them just as they are. I couldn't possibly fit every single seasonal ingredient into this book and nor would I want to. You will find your own seasons for certain recipes, too, I'm sure, and, depending on your climate, food will be cooked at other times of the year. You be the judge; these recipes are yours now.

My year is punctuated by the comings and goings of ingredients. Yes, we have four seasons, but in truth there are all of these micro seasons where ingredients appear and are gone again in blink-and-you'll-miss-it moments to make way for others. While this book is divided into four chapters, it could have easily been several more. Early and late summer are distinctively different, and that period in spring when it finally begins to warm sees the markets exploding with new produce. The nuances of the seasons are what excite me in the kitchen and encourage me to enjoy these precious seasonal windows while we can. Going without something for nine months of the year and then indulging in it for three is an incredible thing. When cherries begin to appear, I get a sort of giddy feeling knowing that holidays and festive eating are approaching. Summer's first peach, mango and nectarine are events, just like the arrival of persimmons and chestnuts in autumn. This is how our grandparents and their parents ate, but that is so easily forgotten. It is time to return to the seasons, cook simply and celebrate the beauty of food.

The recipes in this book are ones I treasure and love to cook at home, and it is the great ingredients that really make them come to life. My recipes are just a guide and I don't like to complicate things too much. There are plenty of quick recipes and some that require more time or ingredients, but are by no means difficult. Overall, the recipes in this book are all linked by taste and pleasure. Whoever it is you cook for – friends, family, yourself – we must remember this: good food tastes delicious, is enjoyable to eat and a joy to prepare.

THE JOY OF A WELL-STOCKED PANTRY

Having a pantry well stocked with non-perishables makes cooking so much simpler and allows you plenty of freedom to alter recipes or make changes to your liking. There is no need to buy everything at once, but with each recipe you make, you begin to accumulate almost all that you need. Over time, I'll find I have ingredients I haven't used in a while. I'll try and use them all up, but see it as a sign that I don't really need those ingredients and so won't buy them again. It's a revolving door and you can't store every single ingredient in your home, so it's about making choices to suit you. Once I come home with my fresh produce, it is rare that I will need to go out again to shop for particular pantry items. While this list is not all encompassing, it is a indication of what my pantry usually looks like – chaotic, but well stocked.

- Anchovies: I buy these in small tins rather than large jars. They are usually better quality, which means they are great to eat as they are as well as being used in cooking.

- Capers: I prefer them in salt rather than in a brine. Simply rinse off the coarse salt before using or soak them in warm water to dissolve the salt before draining.

- Chocolate: Good-quality milk and dark chocolate (50–70 per cent cocoa). I prefer Valrhona and Callebaut.

- Cocoa powder: A nice unsweetened cocoa powder is great for cakes. The best ones are rich and dark in colour. As with chocolate, I like to use Valrhona and Callebaut.

- Dried and canned beans and legumes: Chickpeas, borlotti beans, cannellini beans, split peas and green lentils.

- Dried pasta: I adore the Martelli brand from Tuscany, but there are many great brands, especially from in and around Gragnano near Naples. Buy the best you can afford.

- Dried porcini mushrooms

- Flour:

  - Manitoba flour: A flour which has a particularly high protein content that is especially useful for doughs that require long leavening periods. I use a percentage of it in certain breads and baked goods, such as the brioche on page 75.

  - Semolina flour (*semola di grano duro rimacinata*) is becoming more readily available from specialty grocers. It is made from hard durum wheat, milled to the texture of fine sand.

It has a soft buttery colour and is the flour to use for most hand-rolled pasta shapes that originate from southern Italy. It is very different from the coarse semolina that is commonly found in supermarkets.

- Tipo 00 is a finely milled flour. It is the most refined of all the Italian flours and thus has the least amount of fibre/bran remaining. I use it for making fresh pasta and some baked goods, like the brioche on page 75. Tipo 00 flour is available from most supermarkets and specialty grocers.

- Tipo 0 flour is a little harder to find, but is great for breads as it has a slightly higher protein percentage than 00 and a greater percentage of the whole grain included. If you can't find it, look for strong, bread or baker's flour.

- Good-quality jarred or canned whole tomatoes: I make sure to never run out of this absolute essential in the kitchen as they are the backbone of many of the dishes I cook. There are plenty of ethical issues in the production of tomatoes so be sure to buy a brand you trust.

- Mirin: A rice wine similar to saké, but much sweeter and with lower alcohol content. It's essential to many Japanese dishes.

- Miso paste: There are many varieties of miso paste, which in its most common form is soy beans fermented with rice, koji and salt. It can also be made with barley and, more recently outside of Japan, with legumes such as chickpeas. I mostly use white or red miso paste. White is mild and sweet whereas red has a deeper and more intense flavour. Miso made in small batches by artisans – which is incomparable in flavour to mass-produced varieties – is starting to become more readily available in Japanese and select grocers here in Australia. Miso paste is the base of miso soup, but it also makes an incredible marinade or addition to dressings. One of my favourite snacks is a little miso paste spread on celery sticks!

- Nuts: Almonds, hazelnuts, pine nuts and walnuts are a nice start. Just remember that nuts have a season, too. Fresh and local nuts are best. Avoid imported nuts if you can, as they have usually been in storage for long periods of time and can taste bitter.

- Olive oil: Always extra virgin, and again, buy the best quality you can afford, or buy two different bottles – one for cooking and a superior flavoured (usually more expensive) one for dressing or seasoning. Unlike wine, olive oil doesn't improve with age and is at its best soon after pressing. Look at the pressing dates on a bottle rather than a best-before date as the latter tells you little about its quality. For these reasons, I do prefer local olive oil, but at the end of the season when new-season oils are arriving from Italy and Spain, I will use these, too.

- Olives: Green and black. I love manzanillo and taggiasche olives, respectively.

- Parmesan and pecorino: Although not technically pantry items, you'll always find a wedge of parmigiano reggiano, grana padano and pecorino romano in my fridge. Buy the best you can afford.

- Rice and grains:

  - Carnaroli or Vialone Nano, for risotto
  - Koshihikari, a short-grain Japanese variety
  - Short-grain brown rice
  - Farro, barley, bulgur, quinoa and freekeh.

- Saké: I use regular drinking saké for cooking, albeit a less expensive one than those we buy for actual drinking. Cooking saké is fine too; it has a small amount of salt added to it to prevent it from being consumed as a beverage, and can therefore be sold in shops without a liquor licence.

- Salt: Flaky sea salt has a flavour and texture that I prefer for seasoning and is especially lovely to finish dishes. I use fine sea salt for seasoning the water for pasta or for dough or in baking as it dissolves much easier.

- Sesame oil: An absolute staple in our cupboard. It's deeply roasted and you only need a small amount to flavour a dish. Like soy sauce, try to buy the best quality you can find.

- Soy sauce: I prefer to use light soy over the dark varieties as it is easier to control the flavour and is slightly more subtle, but regular soy is perfectly fine, too. Try to buy soy sauce from a Japanese grocer if you can. Small-batch soy sauce is really something special and definitely worth seeking out if you can.

- Spices: I prefer to purchase spices whole, then toast and grind them myself with a mortar and pestle. They stay fresh longer and have a more intense flavour. The exception is cinnamon, which I keep both whole and ground. My most-used spices are cumin, coriander seeds, cardamom, cinnamon, nutmeg, fennel seeds, chilli flakes and pepper. On that note, I definitely do treat pepper as a spice, rather than a general seasoning like salt. Salt brings out the flavour of food whereas pepper brings heat and spice and, in my opinion, should not be automatically added to all dishes.

- Sugar: Caster, brown, raw and demerara.

- Vanilla: Vanilla extract (not essence), vanilla bean paste and vanilla pods. Once I've scraped the seeds from the pods, I put the pods in a jar filled with rum to make my own vanilla extract, or insert them into a jar filled with caster sugar for fragrant vanilla sugar.

- Vinegar:

  - Aged balsamic vinegar – I mostly use mine for drizzling over ice cream or strawberries, but I also use it occasionally on salads (usually ones with radicchio) and sometimes in a ragù at the last minute for some sweetness.

  - Red wine vinegar, my most commonly used vineagr, for dressings and to give dishes like my Peperonata (page 34) a lift at the end.

  - Rice or grain vinegar – another essential in Japanese cooking. Again, the quality varies immensely so seek out a good-quality one from a Japanese grocer if possible.

FOR THE LOVE
OF LEMONS AND
FRAGRANT HERBS

I am compelled to give a special mention to lemons and fresh herbs.
Knowing I have herbs in the garden and lemons on the bench provides
certainty in the kitchen that a meal can be made. They add freshness
and life. Lemons, especially, are an absolute staple – the zest for
cakes, the juice for dressings and wedges to serve alongside meat
and fish. I implore you to be liberal with your lemons and to always
have them on hand. They will transform many a dish, from dull to
extraordinary. Similarly with herbs, I grew up with food in which herbs
were more than just a garnish. They were bought in large bunches and
used up entirely in just a day. I have to admit I haven't been a very
successful gardener thus far, but I do always grow herbs. They're one
of the most important ingredients in my kitchen and I love being
able to walk outside and pick an array of fresh herbs: parsley, mint,
basil, coriander, sage, oregano, rosemary and thyme. I use herbs
in salads, as seasoning for stock or stirred through sauces –
they almost always improve my cooking.

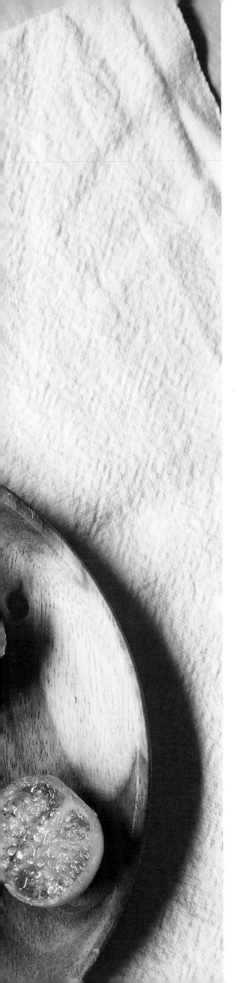

ESSENTIAL KITCHEN ITEMS

My kitchen is tiny. There is no room for unnecessary gadgets cluttering up precious bench space. But regardless of the size, I see no point in accruing items that are only used occasionally (with two exceptions: my ice-cream maker and cherry pitter). I don't like having too many of the one thing either. A few sturdy pots, utensils and a good knife are really all you need to make a delicious meal. Too many kitchen items complicates things, and nobody needs overcomplication in their kitchen. Here is a list of my go-tos – it's not all-encompassing, but covers the items I use most often.

- balloon whisk
- colander and fine-mesh sieve
- digital scales
- electric stand mixer
- food processor (not essential but definitely handy)
- food thermometer for deep-frying
- good-quality kitchen and paring knives
- heavy-based frying pan

- measuring jug
- Microplane zester
- mixing bowls
- mortar and pestle
- pastry brush
- spatulas
- sturdy cast-iron pot
- wire rack for draining deep-fried foods and cooling cakes
- wooden spoons

TECHNICAL THINGS

Oven temperatures given in my recipes are for a conventional oven. If using a fan-forced oven, reduce the temperature by 10–20°C (check your oven manual for best advice).

When cooking pasta, use 2½ teaspoons of salt per litre of water. Add the salt once the water is at a rolling boil and just before you are ready to cook the pasta.

Parsley is always flat-leaf/Italian.

Eggs are always free range and preferably organic, weighing 58–60 g per egg.

SUMMER

I adore the abundance that summer brings. While it can often be too hot to cook, I still find myself wanting to spend the whole summer in the kitchen making the most of the precious summer fruits and vegetables. I bake early in the morning or late in the evening to avoid the heat of the day. All through the season, the house is filled with the aromas of mangoes and apricots in the fruit bowl and tomatoes and basil in the garden. Friends are over more often. We eat outdoors and the pace is slower. The hours between meals blur into whole days of feasting. It is a wonderful time of the year and one I cherish for the long days and plenty of time spent with family.

A breakfast for the weekend, when the only pressing task is brewing the coffee. Crêpes are so versatile and can be topped with whatever fruit you have on hand, or, if things are a little bare, a sprinkling of sugar and a squeeze of lemon juice will do the trick nicely, too. Here, I've suggested whipped ricotta, which I spread thinly on each crêpe, fill with late-summer berries and fold.

One of the things I love most about crêpes is that the batter is best made the night before, so when you wake up you can have crêpes on the table in no time at all. It feels so much more relaxing when the preparation and the eating are far apart in time. You've forgotten the effort you went to and are rewarded for it. If you don't have time for the suggested minimum two hours resting, the crêpes are still delicious even if you rest the batter for just 20 minutes.

CRÊPES WITH WHIPPED RICOTTA

SERVES 4

250 g (1⅔ cups) plain flour, sifted

550 ml full-cream milk

2 eggs

1 tablespoon caster sugar

pinch of fine sea salt

1 teaspoon ground cinnamon

1 vanilla pod, split and seeds scraped, or 1 teaspoon vanilla extract

100 g unsalted butter, melted and cooled, plus extra for cooking

fresh or thawed frozen berries of your choice, to serve

honey or maple syrup, to serve

WHIPPED RICOTTA

300 g fresh full-fat ricotta

1 tablespoon caster sugar

finely grated zest of 1 lemon or orange

pinch of ground cinnamon

Mix together the flour, milk, eggs, sugar, salt, cinnamon and vanilla until smooth. Add the melted butter and mix until well combined. (I do this in a blender, but you can whisk by hand in a large bowl). The batter should be quite runny, almost the consistency of thickened cream. If necessary, transfer to a container or jug, cover and allow to rest in the fridge for at least 2 hours or ideally overnight.

For the whipped ricotta, simply whisk the ingredients together in a large bowl until smooth. Transfer to a serving dish and set aside.

Warm a large non-stick frying pan or crêpe pan over a medium heat and, when hot but not smoking, add a little butter. When foaming, pour in about ¼ cup of the batter and immediately swirl the pan to spread the batter thinly over the base (or, if using a traditional crêpe pan, use the wooden tool to create the crêpe). Cook for just a minute, then flip using a spatula and cook the other side for 30 seconds. The crêpe should be golden and just cooked through. Transfer to a serving plate and keep warm. Repeat with the remaining batter, greasing the pan with extra butter when needed.

Serve the crêpes with the whipped ricotta, topped with berries and honey or maple syrup.

NOTES: Often we'll only use half the batter and store the rest in the fridge for the following morning; it may just need to be thinned out with a little milk the next day.

While a proper crêpe pan does make things easier, if you don't have one, any large frying pan will do.

When your tomatoes are a little lacklustre, slow-roasting them is the key to coaxing out flavour and an intense sweetness that can often be missing. The almonds and mint are crushed into a rough pesto of sorts, which coats the tomatoes and mozzarella, making for one of my favourite summer salads. If I want to bulk the salad out a little, a handful of rocket is a lovely addition.

SLOW-ROASTED TOMATOES WITH MINT AND MOZZARELLA

SERVES 4

800 g roma tomatoes, halved

extra-virgin olive oil,
for drizzling

sea salt

60 g blanched almonds

large handful of mint leaves,
plus extra to garnish

1 small garlic clove, peeled

150 g buffalo mozzarella, torn

Preheat the oven to 160°C. Line a baking tray with baking paper.

Arrange the tomatoes on the tray. Drizzle generously with olive oil and scatter with salt. Roast for 1–1½ hours until the tomatoes are soft and beginning to look a little dried. Set aside to cool.

Meanwhile, pound the almonds to a rough paste using a mortar and pestle. Add the mint and continue to pound. Add the garlic and a pinch of salt and keep pounding until everything is well combined. Stream in some olive oil – just enough to make a spoonable paste. Season to taste and set aside.

Arrange the tomatoes on a serving plate and top with the mozzarella. Spoon over the almond mixture, scatter with extra mint and serve.

Originating in Tuscany, pici are a like a fat spaghetti. The exact recipe for the dough varies from family to family – sometimes made with semolina flour, sometimes with an egg added. They are very textural and so comforting to eat. There are a few sauces that traditionally accompany this pasta shape – most often a simple garlicky tomato one but also one of toasted breadcrumbs – which are both delicious. However, I've been making variations of this lemon sauce since I was 16, after reading a similar recipe in a River Cafe cookbook. The sauce doesn't even need its own pan – it is simply warmed over the pot as the pasta is cooking – making for a simple meal that doesn't require you to stand at the stove for long periods of time (a task no one appreciates in the middle of summer). I have had great success using a combination of pure cream and mascarpone, and an equally fine substitute is, of course, dried pici, spaghetti or bucatini (use 320 grams for four people). I like my sauce quite zingy, so I've left the amount of lemon up to you to adjust – start with one lemon and add the rest if you like.

PICI WITH LEMON MASCARPONE

SERVES 4

finely grated zest of 1 lemon

juice of 1–2 lemons

70 g finely grated parmesan, plus extra to serve

150 g mascarpone

2 tablespoons extra-virgin olive oil

sea salt and black pepper

basil leaves, to serve

PICI

400 g tipo 00 flour

fine sea salt

1 tablespoon extra-virgin olive oil

200 ml warm water

semolina flour (see page 12), for dusting

To make the pici dough, tip the flour onto a clean work surface and mix with a large pinch of salt. Make a well in the centre, add the olive oil and slowly pour in the warm water. Depending on the flour, you may not need to use as much as 200 ml. Use your hands to bring the flour into the water, mixing until you have a rough dough. Knead for about 10 minutes, until smooth. Cover with plastic wrap or an upturned bowl and set aside for at least 30 minutes.

Roll out the dough to a disc around 1 cm thick and then cut the dough into 1 cm strips. Roll each strip into a thin rope around 5 mm wide. The strips will all be varying lengths, but this doesn't matter – the beauty of this pasta is the rustic nature. If the remaining dough begins to dry out, you can rub some olive oil into the surface; alternatively, simply cover the dough with plastic wrap or a clean tea towel. Place the rolled pici on a clean tea towel dusted with semolina flour and continue with the remaining dough.

Bring a large saucepan of water to the boil.

In a large heatproof bowl that will fit over your pasta pan, whisk together the lemon zest and juice, parmesan, mascarpone and olive oil. Taste to see if you need to add more lemon – it should be tangy but not too strong. Season with salt and pepper. Place the bowl over the pot and stir, gently warming the mascarpone mixture for 3–4 minutes until it emulsifies and becomes a homogenous, slightly thickened sauce. Set aside.

Generously salt the boiling water, add the pasta and stir briefly. Cook the pasta for 7–8 minutes until al dente. The pici should be chewy but not chalky. If you find that the sauce has cooled down too much while the pasta is cooking, place the bowl over the boiling water for a minute just before the pasta is done.

Drain the pasta, reserving 250 ml (1 cup) of the cooking water. Add the pici and most of the cooking water to the sauce and stir to coat. It may seem too runny to begin with, but the hot pasta will quickly take up all of the sauce. If the sauce begins to look dry, add the remaining cooking water, a little at a time, until the sauce is nice and creamy again.

Scatter with basil leaves and extra parmesan and serve immediately.

I adore the combination of fish, tomato and mint, which is a common flavour set in Maltese cooking. *Cencioni* (meaning 'little rags') are a flat, oval-shaped pasta with a rough texture. They should be a little rustic and irregular in shape as they are usually made by hand with just a flat knife and a little time. Here the cencioni can be substituted with store-bought dried orecchiette or strascinati, which are very similar in shape. You'll need 320 grams for four people.

CENCIONI WITH TOMATO, FISH AND MINT

SERVES 4

2 tablespoons extra-virgin olive oil

2 garlic cloves, sliced

250 g cherry tomatoes, halved

300 g skinless fillets of firm white fish, such as snapper, blue eye or coral trout, cut into 3 cm pieces

100 ml dry white wine

sea salt

small handful of mint leaves, shredded, plus extra to serve

finely grated lemon zest, to serve

CENCIONI

400 g semolina flour (see page 12), plus extra for dusting

180 ml warm water

fine sea salt

To make the dough for the cencioni, tip the flour onto a clean work surface and mix with a large pinch of salt. Make a well in the centre and slowly pour in the warm water. Use your hands to slowly bring the flour into the water, mixing until you have a rough dough. If the dough feels very dry or difficult to bring together, sprinkle over a little extra water. Knead for about 10 minutes, until smooth. It should be soft but not sticky. Add extra semolina flour if necessary. Cover with plastic wrap or an upturned bowl and set aside for at least 30 minutes.

Take a small piece of the dough, keeping the remainder covered while you work, and roll into a rope about 1.5 cm wide. Cut the rope into 1.5 cm pieces and, using a flat butter knife angled at 45 degrees, drag the piece of dough across your work surface. It should be mostly flat with a little texture. Place the cencioni on a clean tea towel dusted with semolina flour and continue with the remaining dough.

Heat the olive oil in a large frying pan over a low–medium heat and gently fry the garlic and tomatoes until the tomatoes are beginning to blister and release some liquid. Add the fish and cook for a minute, then add the wine and simmer gently for 3–4 minutes until the fish is just cooked through, stirring occasionally – be gentle so you don't break up the fish. Season with salt to taste.

Meanwhile, bring a large saucepan of water to the boil. Generously salt the water, add the pasta and cook for 4–5 minutes or until just under al dente. Drain, reserving 250 ml (1 cup) of the cooking water. Increase the heat to medium and add the pasta to the sauce, along with some of the cooking water if the sauce is a little dry. Cook for 1–2 minutes until the pasta is well coated, adding more water if necessary. Stir through the mint, then sprinkle with the lemon zest and extra mint and serve.

When we think of pesto, it's usually the one made with pine nuts, basil and parmesan. That particular pesto is from Genova and consequently is called pesto alla genovese. While it's probably the most famous one, it's not the only pesto out there. Pesto is simply something that is crushed, ground or pounded (coming from the Italian verb *pestare* meaning exactly that: to crush, grind or pound). When you know that, I think it gives you a lot of freedom. I make pesto with walnuts, parsley, pistachios, mint – whatever I have that will work.

One of my absolute favourite kinds of pesto is this one, pesto alla trapanese, hailing from Trapani in Sicily. It's a summer staple in our house for its freshness and ease. Traditionally, this pesto is paired with a spiral pasta shape called busiate, but any spiral pasta is lovely. Instead of parmesan, top the pasta with crunchy breadcrumbs, known as *formaggio dei poveri* or 'poor man's cheese'. If I don't have any basil, I'll substitute mint, which is lovely here, too.

I make my pesto with a mortar and pestle. It truly only takes five or so minutes and, in my opinion, gives much better results. It can, of course, be made in a food processor – just use the pulse button to avoid making it too smooth, as it should still have some texture. There's no need to add each ingredient separately as I suggest for the mortar and pestle, just throw it all in then loosen with the oil at the end.

BUSIATE WITH PESTO ALLA TRAPANESE

SERVES 4

6 roma tomatoes

70 g blanched almonds, lightly toasted

large handful of basil leaves

2 garlic cloves, peeled

sea salt

100–150 ml extra-virgin olive oil

320 g busiate or dried pasta of your choice

CRUNCHY BREADCRUMBS

2 tablespoons olive oil

100 g fresh breadcrumbs (see Note)

sea salt

Using a small, sharp knife, cut a cross at the base of each tomato. Blanch in a large saucepan of boiling water for 1 minute, then drain. When cool enough to handle, peel and halve each tomato. Scrape out the seeds and remove the core (keep the insides to add to soups or sauces, as you won't need them for this dish). Roughly chop the tomato flesh and set aside.

Pound the almonds using a mortar and pestle. Add the basil and continue to pound so that the almonds and basil start to form a coarse paste. Now add the garlic, along with a large pinch of salt (this will help the garlic to break down more easily) and crush the garlic into the basil and almonds. It should be smelling heavenly at this point. Once you are happy with the texture, tumble in the chopped tomato and gently pound to incorporate it into the pesto. I like my pesto rather chunky, but you can crush it as smooth as you like. Now stir in enough olive oil to make a thick but spoonable pesto. Check for seasoning, adding more salt if needed, and transfer to a large bowl. Set aside.

For the crunchy breadcrumbs, heat the olive oil in a frying pan over a medium heat. Add the breadcrumbs and stir to coat. Cook, stirring often, for about 3 minutes until golden and crunchy. Season with salt and set aside.

Bring a large saucepan of water to the boil. Generously salt the water, add the pasta and cook according to the packet instructions until al dente. Drain, reserving 250 ml (1 cup) of the cooking water. Add the pasta and most of the cooking water to the bowl with the pesto and stir so that everything is well coated. If it looks too dry, add the remaining cooking water. Serve with a generous scattering of the crunchy breadcrumbs.

NOTE: I make my own breadcrumbs from leftover day-old bread. Simply whiz it up in the food processor and store in an airtight container for up to a week or in the freezer for up to 3 months.

Peperonata is such a versatile dish. Served simply with bread, stirred through pasta, as a topping for pizza, stuffed into a panino, served on top of polenta and, maybe most obviously, as a side dish to meat or fish – I especially like it with swordfish. Use red and yellow capsicums for their sweetness and make sure you adjust the seasoning at the end. The splash of vinegar really lifts this peperonata, so although I've suggested two teaspoons, don't be afraid to add more to achieve the right balance.

PEPERONATA

SERVES 4

2 tablespoons extra-virgin olive oil

1 onion, finely sliced

2 garlic cloves, finely sliced

800 g capsicums (a mixture of red and yellow), trimmed and sliced into 1 cm strips

400 g canned whole peeled tomatoes

pinch of caster sugar

2 oregano sprigs or a small handful of basil leaves

sea salt

2 teaspoons red wine vinegar, plus extra if needed

Heat the olive oil in a heavy-based saucepan over a low–medium heat. Gently fry the onion and garlic for 10–15 minutes until softened and just beginning to colour. Increase the heat to medium and add the sliced capsicum, stirring it through the onion and garlic. Add the tomatoes, sugar and herbs and simmer for 30–35 minutes, stirring occasionally and breaking up the tomatoes with the back of a wooden spoon, until the capsicum has softened and the sauce has reduced. Season with salt and stir through the vinegar. Taste and add more sugar, salt or vinegar if necessary. You can serve immediately, otherwise the peperonata will keep in an airtight container in the fridge for up to 5 days.

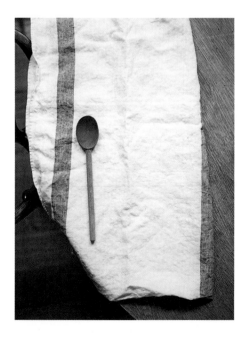

Miso paste is one of our fridge staples. I use it, of course, for miso soup, but also in marinades, as a snack spread on crunchy vegetables, and in dressings, as I've done here. This salad is fresh, punchy and salty. The miso brings more than salt though – it has a sweet, rounded flavour, which is irreplaceable.

GREEN BEAN AND RADISH SALAD WITH MISO DRESSING

SERVES 4

850 g green beans, trimmed

1 bunch of radishes, trimmed and quartered

2 tablespoons toasted white sesame seeds

MISO DRESSING

1 heaped tablespoon miso paste (any variety)

3 tablespoons sesame oil

1 tablespoon soy sauce, plus extra if needed

1 tablespoon rice wine vinegar, plus extra if needed

1 teaspoon caster sugar, plus extra if needed

pinch of sea salt, plus extra if needed

Blanch the beans in a large saucepan of boiling water. Drain and refresh in cold water. Place the radishes in a salad bowl along with the beans and sesame seeds. Toss to combine.

Meanwhile, for the dressing, whisk all of the ingredients together in a bowl. Check for seasoning – it should be well balanced with sweetness, saltiness and sharpness so add more soy, salt, vinegar or sugar as required – then pour over the beans and radishes. Mix well and serve.

When zucchini first appear at the markets, I am thrilled, but after a month or two, I feel like I have used up all of my zucchini-based ideas. I do love zucchini though, so I persevere, knowing they won't be abundant for much longer. This recipe was inspired in part by a dish I ate in Rome – grilled, finely sliced and marinated zucchini served with mozzarella on top of crostini – and equally inspired by the desire to not give up on the glut of zucchini that summer brings. Here, they're grilled then marinated, draped over a bed of stracciatella and topped with walnuts. Stracciatella is, basically speaking, the soft filling inside burrata: shredded fresh mozzarella mixed with cream. It is milky and creamy, and great on top of pasta, too. If you can't find stracciatella, substitute burrata or slices of buffalo mozzarella.

MARINATED ZUCCHINI WITH WALNUTS AND STRACCIATELLA

SERVES 4

4 small zucchini (650 g), halved lengthways then cut into 4 cm pieces

80 ml (⅓ cup) extra-virgin olive oil, plus extra to serve

sea salt

3 marjoram or oregano sprigs, leaves picked

3 tablespoons red wine vinegar

150 g stracciatella

50 g walnuts, toasted and roughly chopped

mint leaves, to serve

crusty bread, to serve (optional)

In a bowl, combine the zucchini with 2 tablespoons of the olive oil and a good pinch of salt.

Heat a large frying pan over a high heat and cook the zucchini for 5–7 minutes until tender and golden on all sides. Return to the bowl, add the marjoram or oregano and pour over the vinegar and remaining 2 tablespoons of olive oil. Toss to combine and set aside to marinate for 5 minutes.

Spoon the stracciatella onto a small serving plate. Top with the zucchini and scatter over the walnuts and mint leaves. Drizzle over a little extra olive oil and serve with crusty bread to mop up all the juices, if desired.

I make a version of this salad almost every week. Sometimes with a dressing of fish sauce, lime, garlic and chilli; sometimes with tofu instead of chicken and with whatever suitable herbs I have. The dressing is what really makes this salad pop, though – it's creamy and sweet and sour, and ties everything together. If you want to make this salad even quicker, leftover roast chicken can be shredded and tossed through instead of poaching your own.

POACHED CHICKEN VERMICELLI NOODLE SALAD

SERVES 4

2 skinless chicken breast fillets (about 500 g in total)

2 cm piece of ginger, sliced

100 ml saké

200 g rice vermicelli noodles

2 small carrots or 1 large, julienned

1 granny smith apple, julienned

large handful of mint leaves, torn

large handful of coriander leaves, torn

60 g roasted salted peanuts

2 red shallots, halved and finely sliced

COCONUT–GINGER DRESSING

125 ml (½ cup) coconut cream

1 tablespoon fish sauce

generous pinch of sea salt

juice of 2 limes, plus extra if needed

1 teaspoon caster sugar, plus extra if needed

1 cm piece of ginger, finely grated

1 bird's eye chilli, finely sliced

Place the chicken breasts in a medium saucepan and cover with cold water. Add the ginger and saké and bring to the boil over a high heat. Reduce the heat and gently simmer, covered, for approximately 10 minutes. Allow to cool in the liquid for 15 minutes. Remove the chicken, shred the meat and set aside.

Cook the noodles according to the packet instructions, refresh in cold water, then drain. Combine the carrot, apple, mint, coriander, peanuts, shallot, noodles and shredded chicken in a large bowl.

To make the dressing, whisk all the ingredients together in a small bowl and taste to make sure that it is balanced. It should be nice and bright from the lime with a good amount of saltiness and subtle sweetness – adjust the seasoning if you need to. Pour the dressing over the salad and toss well to ensure everything is thoroughly coated. Check again for seasoning and serve.

Yellow and red capsicums are the best for this dish as green ones can be incredibly bitter, especially once cooked. I love to eat these as an outdoor lunch with a crisp green salad – they're also great as a side to grilled or roasted meat. These are best eaten as soon as they come out of the oven, while the mozzarella is still soft and milky.

STUFFED PEPPERS

SERVES 4

4 large red or yellow capsicums (or a mixture of both)

300 g fresh breadcrumbs (see Note page 33)

1 tablespoon salted capers, rinsed, patted dry and roughly chopped

2 garlic cloves, finely chopped or grated

finely grated zest of 1 lemon

handful of parsley leaves, finely chopped

80 ml (⅓ cup) extra-virgin olive oil, plus extra for drizzling

200 g buffalo mozzarella, torn or sliced into pieces

8 anchovy fillets

lemon wedges, to serve

Preheat the oven to 180°C. Grease a large baking tray with a little olive oil.

Cut the capsicums in half lengthways and remove any seeds and white pith, while keeping the stalks intact (this will hold everything together as they roast). Arrange the capsicum halves, cut-side up, on the prepared tray. If they are not sitting flat, slice off the smallest amount to create a flat bottom, ensuring you don't cut through the flesh and create a hole.

Place the breadcrumbs in a large bowl with the capers, garlic, lemon zest and parsley. Drizzle in the olive oil and mix to combine.

Place pieces of mozzarella inside each capsicum half and top with an anchovy fillet. Divide the stuffing among the capsicums and drizzle with a little more olive oil. Roast for about 25 minutes, until the capsicums have collapsed and are beginning to char in places.

Allow to cool slightly, then serve with lemon wedges.

When it's just too hot to cook, this is dinner. So simple but so tasty – just marinated trout with other bits and pieces to add flavour and texture. You can use salmon or tuna instead of trout if you prefer, but be sure it's sashimi grade – ask your fishmonger what they recommend on the day.

TROUT RICE BOWLS

SERVES 4

250 g short-grain rice

400 g sashimi-grade skinless ocean trout, cut into 2 cm cubes

1 spring onion, finely sliced, plus extra to serve

1 Lebanese cucumber, finely diced

3 radishes, finely diced

3 tablespoons soy sauce

2 tablespoons mirin

2 tablespoons rice wine vinegar

2 teaspoons sesame oil

2 cm piece of ginger, finely grated

100 g podded edamame, blanched and refreshed

toasted sesame seeds, to serve

Rinse the rice well, then transfer to a saucepan. Cover with 375 ml (1½ cups) of cold water and place over a high heat. Bring to the boil and cook for 2 minutes. Reduce the heat to low, cover with a tight-fitting lid and cook for a further 10–12 minutes. Turn off the heat and leave the rice to sit, covered, for 10 minutes to absorb any remaining liquid. (Alternatively, use a rice cooker or follow the packet instructions – see Note.)

Combine the trout, spring onion, cucumber and radish in a bowl.

In a small bowl, whisk together the soy, mirin, vinegar, sesame oil and grated ginger. Pour over the trout mixture and stir well to coat. Set aside to marinate for 5 minutes.

Divide the rice among bowls, then top with the trout mixture. Scatter over the edamame, sesame seeds and extra spring onion and serve.

NOTE: I use a stovetop clay pot to cook rice at home, so exact cooking times may vary depending on the size and kind of pot you use. If in doubt, follow the packet directions or the instructions on your particular rice cooker.

This fresh and vibrant pasta takes no time at all to make. There is something a little romantic about seafood with pasta – it makes me feel like I'm on holiday. Roughly chopping the prawns helps intensify the flavour through the sauce and means you get some with each mouthful of the spaghetti. If your fennel doesn't have many fronds, you may want to stir through some finely chopped parsley at the end.

SPAGHETTI WITH FENNEL AND PRAWNS

SERVES 4

100 ml extra-virgin olive oil, plus extra to serve

1 fennel bulb, finely chopped and fronds reserved

sea salt

250 g cherry tomatoes, halved

4 garlic cloves, finely chopped

¼ teaspoon fennel seeds, roughly ground

½ teaspoon dried chilli flakes

320 g dried spaghetti or spaghetti alla chitarra (see Note)

300 g raw prawn meat, roughly chopped

juice of ½ lemon

Heat the olive oil in a large frying pan over a low–medium heat. Gently fry the fennel with a pinch of salt for around 10 minutes, stirring occasionally, until soft and aromatic. Add the cherry tomatoes, garlic, fennel seeds and chilli flakes and cook for around 4 minutes, until the tomatoes are beginning to soften. Use the back of a wooden spoon to help the tomatoes burst a little from their skins. The sauce at this stage should be jammy and thick. Turn off the heat.

Meanwhile, cook the pasta in a large saucepan of generously salted boiling water for a minute or two less than the cooking time instructed on the packet, until just under al dente. Drain, reserving 250 ml (1 cup) of the cooking water.

A few minutes before the pasta is cooked, turn the heat under the sauce to high, add the prawn meat and cook for about 2 minutes until just opaque. Add the cooked spaghetti and most of the cooking water and cook, stirring continuously, for a few minutes longer or until the pasta is al dente. If the sauce begins to look dry, add the remaining cooking water. Stir through the reserved fennel fronds and the lemon juice, and serve with an extra drizzle of olive oil.

NOTE: Spaghetti alla chitarra is a square spaghetti from Abruzzo. It is similar to tonnarelli, which comes from Lazio. Both can be found in select Italian delis and grocers.

My variations on this salad change throughout the year. When the potatoes are new and the fennel is abundant in late summer and early autumn, this is the one I like to prepare. The preserved lemon is optional if you're making the mayonnaise for another purpose, but absolutely use it in this dish as it's really what makes it. You can substitute store-bought mayonnaise, then simply stir in the preserved lemon.

LEMONY POTATO AND FENNEL SALAD

SERVES 6

1 kg dutch cream or other waxy potatoes

70 ml extra-virgin olive oil

2 tablespoons salted capers, rinsed and patted dry

150 g plain full-fat yoghurt

finely grated zest and juice of 1 lemon

sea salt

handful of mint leaves, roughly chopped

handful of parsley leaves, roughly chopped

handful of basil leaves, roughly chopped

1 small fennel bulb, finely sliced and fronds roughly chopped

MAYONNAISE (MAKES ABOUT 375 G/1½ CUPS)

1 egg

300 ml vegetable oil

2 tablespoons white wine vinegar

1 tablespoon dijon mustard

½ preserved lemon, rinsed, flesh discarded and rind very finely chopped (optional)

sea salt

Boil the potatoes in generously salted water for 15–20 minutes, depending on size, until very tender. Drain and cool, then cut into 3 cm pieces.

Meanwhile, heat 1 tablespoon of the olive oil in a small frying pan over a medium heat and fry the capers for about 2 minutes until crispy. Allow to cool.

To make the mayonnaise, place the egg in a food processor. With the motor running, add the oil in a thin stream until the mixture is pale and thick. Add the vinegar, mustard and preserved lemon (if using) and continue to process until combined. Season to taste. The mayonnaise can be made ahead of time. Store in an airtight container in the fridge for 2–3 days.

Place 160 g (⅔ cup) of the mayonnaise in a bowl (reserve the remaining mayonnaise for another use). Add the yoghurt, lemon zest and juice and the remaining 2½ tablespoons of olive oil, whisk together and season to taste.

Combine the potatoes in a large bowl with the herbs, fennel and most of the capers. Pour the dressing over the top and mix well to combine. Scatter over the remaining crispy capers and serve.

In Malta, it is traditional to stuff fish this way, and my mother often makes this stuffed snapper for Christmas. Here, I've rested it on a bed of potato, fennel and shallot for a complete meal. One large snapper is the norm in our family, but smaller ones are often more manageable and look quite lovely, too.

WHOLE STUFFED SNAPPER

SERVES 6

1 x 1.5 kg snapper or 2 x 750 g snapper, cleaned, scaled and gutted

3 large waxy potatoes, finely sliced

1 fennel bulb, finely sliced, fronds roughly chopped and reserved for the stuffing

1 French shallot, sliced

3 tablespoons extra-virgin olive oil

sea salt

lemon wedges, to serve

TOMATO AND HERB STUFFING

2 tomatoes, roughly chopped

large handful of mint leaves, roughly chopped

large handful of parsley leaves, roughly chopped

150 g fresh breadcrumbs (see Note page 33)

1 tablespoon salted capers, rinsed and patted dry

finely grated zest of 1 lemon

3 tablespoons extra-virgin olive oil

sea salt

Preheat the oven to 180°C.

Dry the snapper thoroughly inside and out using paper towel. If using one larger snapper, make sharp cuts in the top of the flesh on one side of the fish to help it cook a little faster.

To make the stuffing, combine the tomato, herbs, breadcrumbs, capers, lemon zest and olive oil in a large bowl with the reserved fennel fronds. Season to taste.

Arrange the potato, fennel and shallot in a large roasting tin and drizzle over 1½ tablespoons of the olive oil. Place the fish on top and then, using your hands, fill the cavity with the stuffing. Drizzle the fish with the remaining 1½ tablespoons of olive oil and season well.

Cover the tray tightly with foil and bake for 20 minutes. Increase the oven temperature to 200°C, remove the foil and bake for 10 more minutes or until the fish is just cooked and the potato is golden. A large snapper may need a little longer so keep checking every 5 minutes after the 30-minute mark. Serve with plenty of lemon wedges.

Ramen can be very time-consuming to prepare and involves putting a lot of effort into the base broth. Here, I suggest a lighter and, by comparison, faster route, which suits us at home. The soup has a chicken base, which means you can use chicken broth from your freezer or store-bought broth. I use bones and pieces for the broth, but a whole chicken works well, too. I make the noodles at home as it can be difficult to source good-quality ramen noodles and I do love the action of making them – but of course you can buy them if you're short on time. Whether you make everything from scratch or take a few short cuts, this is a wonderful version for home and one that won't have you in the kitchen for three days. I like to make double the amount of the tare (seasoning) and top the poached chicken with a small dollop when serving. Another step to add more flavour is to grill the cob of corn until it is slightly charred – it will add a nice smokiness to the ramen once the kernels are in the broth. A little sprinkling of crushed black sesame seeds is nice, too. You'll need to start this recipe the day before to marinate the eggs.

CHICKEN MISO RAMEN

SERVES 4

SOY EGGS

4 eggs

iced water, for refreshing

2½ tablespoons light soy sauce

100 ml mirin

CHICKEN BROTH

1 chicken frame

4 chicken wings

2 bone-in chicken thighs
(about 300 g in total)

3 cm piece of ginger, sliced

2 garlic cloves, bruised

1 spring onion

sea salt

RAMEN NOODLES

400 g (2⅔ cups) plain flour,
plus extra for dusting

1½ teaspoons baking powder

1 tablespoon fine sea salt

2 eggs

2½ tablespoons warm water

CONTINUED OVERLEAF →

For the soy eggs, cook the eggs in a small saucepan of simmering water for 6 minutes. Plunge the eggs into iced water for 3 minutes, then carefully peel and place in a small container. Bring the soy and mirin to a simmer in a small saucepan, then pour over the eggs. Allow to cool, then cover and set aside in the fridge for at least 1 day to marinate.

For the broth, place all the ingredients in a stockpot, cover with 1.2 litres of water and place over a medium heat. Bring to the boil, then reduce the heat and cover so the stock is barely simmering. Skim any impurities from the surface as they arise and cook for 30 minutes. Remove the thighs and reserve, then continue cooking the broth for 1 hour. Strain, discarding the bones and aromatics. You can use the broth immediately or transfer it to an airtight container. It will keep in the fridge for up to 3 days or in the freezer for up to 3 months.

To make the dough for the noodles, tip the flour, baking powder and salt onto a clean work surface and mix with your hands so that everything is evenly distributed. Make a well in the centre and crack in the eggs. Gently whisk the eggs using a fork and drizzle in the warm water. Slowly bring in the flour and mix to incorporate. When the dough becomes stiff, use your hands to bring it together – it shouldn't be too crumbly, but also not sticky. Add a little more water as you need it – every type of flour is different, so go by feel. (Alternatively, mix all of the ingredients together in a food processor until it forms a stiff dough.) Knead for about 10 minutes until the dough is smooth and elastic. Flatten into a disc, cover with a damp cloth or plastic wrap and allow to rest at room temperature for at least 30 minutes.

Divide the noodle dough into four pieces. Cover three of the pieces and set aside. On a lightly floured work surface, use a rolling pin to roll out the dough into a rough disc around 3 mm thick. Roll the dough through a pasta machine set to the widest setting, then continue to roll through the narrower settings until the sheet is 2 mm in thickness. Cut either by hand or using the spaghetti attachment on your machine. Dust with extra flour and set aside. Repeat with the remaining portions of dough.

CONTINUED OVERLEAF →

TARE

100 g white miso paste

1 tablespoon sesame oil,
plus extra if needed

2 teaspoons sugar,
plus extra if needed

2 teaspoons sea salt,
plus extra if needed

2 teaspoons saké,
plus extra if needed

2 teaspoons soy sauce,
plus extra if needed

2.5 cm piece of ginger, grated

2 garlic cloves, grated

TOPPINGS

sliced spring onion

grilled corn kernels

butter

For the tare, simply mix all of the ingredients together in a bowl and check for seasoning. It should be salty and sweet and well balanced. Feel free to add more of the sesame oil, sugar, salt, saké or soy until it is to your liking. Divide the tare among four bowls.

Bring the broth to a simmer and season with salt. Bring a large saucepan of water to the boil for the noodles. Cook the noodles for 4 minutes, or until al dente, then drain. Ladle the hot broth into the bowls, stir to combine with the tare and check for seasoning. Divide the noodles among the bowls. Slice the reserved chicken thighs and cut the soy eggs in half lengthways. Place on top of the noodles, then complete the ramen with the other toppings – plenty of spring onion, corn and a little bit of butter – and serve.

This is one of my favourite meals to make at home and the whole family loves it. Summer cooking should feel easy and effortless and this dish is exactly that. Because the chicken can be marinated overnight, when dinnertime comes, there is hardly anything to do at all. The lactic acid in the yoghurt tenderises the chicken, keeping it nice and juicy as it cooks, and carries all of the other marinade ingredients really well. I've used marylands, which are the thigh and drumstick of the chicken, but either of those pieces separately would be perfect, too. Just make sure they have the skin on and bone in, to prevent the chicken from drying out.

YOGHURT ROAST CHICKEN WITH CUCUMBER SALAD

SERVES 4–6

4 chicken marylands
(about 1.3 kg in total)

250 g (1 cup) plain
full-fat yoghurt

2 tablespoons extra-virgin
olive oil

4 garlic cloves, finely grated

1 teaspoon smoked paprika

1 teaspoon ground coriander

1 teaspoon ground cumin

finely grated zest of 1 lemon

1 bunch of coriander, stalks finely
chopped and leaves reserved

pinch of sea salt

lemon cheeks, to serve

CUCUMBER SALAD

4 Lebanese cucumbers,
roughly chopped

1 small red onion, finely sliced

handful of mint and coriander
leaves, roughly chopped

2 tablespoons extra-virgin
olive oil

juice of ½ lemon

sea salt

1 teaspoon sumac

Place the chicken in a large non-reactive bowl along with the yoghurt, olive oil, garlic, spices, lemon zest, coriander stalks and salt. Using your hands, work the marinade into the chicken, ensuring everything is well mixed and the chicken is completely coated. Cover and leave to marinate in the fridge for at least 30 minutes, but ideally overnight.

Preheat the oven to 190°C.

Arrange the chicken pieces, skin-side up, in a single layer in a shallow roasting dish or tin, pouring any excess marinade on top. Allow the chicken to come back to room temperature, then roast for 40–45 minutes or until the chicken is nicely coloured and cooked through.

Meanwhile, for the salad, combine the cucumber, onion and herbs in a medium bowl. Drizzle over the olive oil and lemon juice and season to taste with salt. Sprinkle over the sumac.

Serve the yoghurt chicken with the cucumber salad and lemon cheeks.

Harissa is an incredibly versatile paste – it can be used simply as a condiment, but it also makes for a great marinade. It has such a pronounced flavour that you really don't need to complicate things and add much else. I've used it here as a marinade for pork cutlets and paired them with a fresh, vibrant salad of peaches, tomato and corn. This is a lovely way to eat during the warmer months.

HARISSA PORK AND A SUMMER SALAD

SERVES 4

4 pork cutlets
(about 250 g each)

2 tablespoons harissa paste

2 tablespoons extra-virgin olive oil

sea salt

PEACH, CORN AND TOMATO SALAD

1 small red onion, finely sliced

sea salt

4 yellow peaches (about 500 g in total), stones removed, cut into wedges

2 corn cobs, blanched, cooled and kernels removed

200 g tomatoes (a mixture of heirloom varieties is nice), roughly chopped

large handful of basil leaves, torn

large handful of mint leaves, torn

3 tablespoons extra-virgin olive oil

juice of 1 lime

Place the pork chops in a large, non-reactive dish or bowl and add the harissa paste, olive oil and a good pinch of salt. Using your hands, massage the paste and oil into the pork. Cover and leave to marinate for at least 20 minutes. If you are marinating for longer, pop it in the fridge, but allow the pork to come to room temperature before cooking.

Meanwhile, for the salad, place the red onion and a large pinch of salt in a small bowl. Rub the salt into the onion and allow to sit for 5 minutes. On a large plate, arrange the peach, corn and tomatoes. Scatter over the herbs and the salted red onion. In a small bowl, whisk together the olive oil and lime juice. Season to taste and drizzle over the salad.

Heat a large frying pan over a medium–high heat or a barbecue grill plate to medium–high and cook the pork chops for about 4 minutes on each side until just cooked through. Make sure you do this in a well-ventilated area as the harissa, once it hits the heat, will give off very strong chilli fumes. If you are particularly sensitive, I would advise using an outdoor barbecue or roasting the cutlets in a 180°C oven for around 20 minutes until just cooked through. Serve with the salad.

This is a simple cake that I love to make in summer. A really good peach is a thing of beauty and makes me feel that summer has truly arrived. Here, I poach them ever so quickly, just to take the fuzzy skin off. The skin is fine if you're eating a peach fresh, but the texture is less desirable when baked. You can use good-quality jarred peaches here, just be sure to pat them dry first.

PEACH, RASPBERRY AND ALMOND CAKE

SERVES 8

150 g unsalted butter, softened

250 g caster sugar

3 eggs

1 teaspoon vanilla extract

finely grated zest of 1 orange

155 g (1½ cups) ground almonds (see Note page 184)

100 g (⅔ cup) self-raising flour, sifted

125 g (1 cup) fresh or thawed frozen raspberries

50 g almonds, roughly chopped

POACHED PEACHES

3 white or yellow peaches (about 500 g in total)

3 tablespoons caster sugar

1 vanilla pod, split and seeds scraped

Preheat the oven to 180°C. Grease a 21 cm round loose-bottomed or springform cake tin with butter and line with baking paper.

To poach the peaches, using a small sharp knife, make a small cross in the base of each peach. Place the sugar and vanilla in a large saucepan with 1 litre of water. Bring to a simmer over a medium heat. Carefully add the peaches and poach gently for 3–5 minutes until the skin looks like it will slip off easily. The purpose of the poaching is to remove the skin, not to cook the peaches, so just keep an eye on them and be conservative with timings so as not to cook them too much – ripe peaches especially may need less time. Remove the peaches with a slotted spoon and allow to cool. Remove the skin and discard. You can keep the poaching liquid for another use. Cut the peaches in half, removing the stone, then slice into 1.5 cm wedges. Set aside.

Cream the butter and sugar together, either using a wooden spoon or a stand mixer fitted with a paddle attachment, until light and fluffy. Add the eggs, one at a time, beating well between each addition. Stir in the vanilla, orange zest and ground almonds, then gently fold in the flour, mixing until just incorporated and smooth.

Pour the batter into the prepared tin. Gently press the raspberries and peach slices into the cake batter, then scatter the almonds around the edge. Bake for 40–45 minutes until a skewer comes out clean when inserted in the centre. Leave to cool in the tin for a few minutes, then transfer to a wire rack to cool completely.

Apricots are the first sign of summer, and I buy them any chance I get. They don't often make it into baked goods – I think they're probably my favourite fruit so I truly just enjoy them as they are. I'm always craving the flavour of the ones I remember eating as a young girl – they taste of childhood and fill me with nostalgia – firm, but so juicy when bitten, and immensely perfumed. When apricots aren't as full of flavour, I prefer to bake with them. It sweetens the fruit and remedies any undesirable texture. My suggestion of apricot and berries for this galette makes it perfect for summer, but in other seasons different fruits can be used – apples, pears and rhubarb are all great. With those fruits I simply scatter some cinnamon sugar over the pastry, top it with thin slices of apple or pear and thicker slices of rhubarb, then scatter with some more sugar and dot with butter. Flour is only necessary for fruit that is very soft and juicy when cooked, such as the apricots and berries here. The pastry is so flaky with very little effort thanks to the sour cream, which provides additional fat and moisture to puff up the layers during the bake.

APRICOT AND BERRY GALETTE

SERVES 8

4 apricots (about 300 g in total), halved and stones removed

250 g mixed fresh or thawed frozen berries, such as blackberries, raspberries and mulberries

1 teaspoon plain flour

3 tablespoons raw sugar

pinch of ground cinnamon

1 vanilla pod, split and seeds scraped, or 1 teaspoon vanilla bean paste

full-cream milk, for brushing

demerara sugar, for sprinkling

double cream, to serve

SOUR CREAM PASTRY

350 g (2⅓ cups) plain flour

1 tablespoon caster sugar

pinch of fine sea salt

150 g chilled unsalted butter, cut into cubes

200 g sour cream

2–3 tablespoons iced water

To make the dough for the pastry, mix the flour, sugar and salt together in a large bowl. Rub the cold butter into the flour using your fingertips or a pastry cutter until you have the texture of coarse breadcrumbs. Some larger pieces of butter are good. Mix in the sour cream and sprinkle in enough iced water to just bring the dough together. Flatten into a disc, wrap and chill in the fridge for at least 1 hour.

Take out the pastry 10 minutes before you want to use it. Line a 25 cm round baking tray with baking paper. Roll out the dough on a lightly floured work surface into a large round about 5 mm thick (it doesn't have to be perfectly round, galettes are meant to be wonderfully rustic). Drape the pastry over the prepared tray. Place the apricots, cut-side down, on the pastry, leaving a border of about 4 cm. In a small bowl, mix the berries with the flour, 1 tablespoon of the raw sugar, the cinnamon and vanilla. Scatter the berries around the apricots, then sprinkle the remaining raw sugar over all of the fruit. Fold in the overhanging pastry edge to create a border, pinching it together at intervals to create a roughly circular shape. Brush the pastry with milk and scatter with a little demerara sugar. Chill in the fridge for 1 hour.

Preheat the oven to 200°C.

Bake the galette for 35–40 minutes until the pastry is golden, the fruit is soft and the are juices bubbling. Allow to cool completely before serving – the juices thicken upon cooling, helping to keep the galette intact when you begin to slice it. The galette will certainly be delicious warm, just be warned that it may be a little too juicy. Serve with a dollop of double cream.

This is one of the most delicious and simple 'cakes': just cream and raspberries sandwiched between biscuits, left to sit in the fridge. Inspired by the chocolate ripple cakes that were so popular during my high school days in the country, this version is considerably lighter and perfect for summer. Because it requires absolutely no cooking, it's my go-to dessert when it's scorching hot. I love serving this over the festive season when berries are juicy and sweet. You'll need to assemble the cake a whole day before you want to eat it.

RASPBERRY RIPPLE CAKE

SERVES 6–8

600 ml pure cream

250 g (1 cup) crème fraîche

1 vanilla pod, split and seeds scraped, or 1 teaspoon vanilla bean paste

40 g (⅓ cup) icing sugar, sifted

250 g (2 cups) raspberries, plus extra to serve

finely grated zest of 1 lemon

250 g Butternut Snap or other plain sweet biscuits

red currants, to serve (optional)

Combine the cream, crème fraîche, vanilla and 3 tablespoons of the icing sugar in a large bowl and whip to stiff peaks.

Place the raspberries in a bowl with the lemon zest and the remaining 1 tablespoon of icing sugar and crush together with the back of a fork.

Line a 23 cm loaf tin with plastic wrap, with plenty overhanging. Spread a thin layer of the whipped cream over the base then top with a layer of biscuits. You can break some of them if you need to make them fit. Top with another layer of the cream, then half of the raspberry mixture. Repeat the layers with the remaining ingredients, finishing with cream (reserve about ½ cup of the cream mixture for finishing the cake). Enclose the cake with the overhanging plastic wrap and place in the freezer overnight. Transfer to the fridge and leave for a further 8–12 hours.

When ready to serve, unwrap the overhanging plastic wrap, pop your serving plate over the tin and invert the whole thing. Lift off the tin and remove the plastic wrap.

Use the remaining cream to cover the sides and top of the cake, then decorate with extra raspberries and some red currants (if using). Serve immediately.

I've always loved the idea of yeasted cakes, which are more like sweet bread than cake and can be topped with a variety of fruits. In Germany, you will find them baked with layers of fruit and a cheese mixture made of quark, and topped with a crunchy streusel layer. This is a very simple version and relies on in-season apricots to accentuate its flavour. Eat this cake warm from the oven or at the very least on the day of baking. As it is a yeasted cake, it will become dry as the days pass.

APRICOT YEASTED CAKE

SERVES 8

150 ml full-cream milk

300 g tipo 00 flour

7 g active dry yeast

pinch of fine sea salt

finely grated zest of 1 lemon

1 egg, lightly beaten

70 g unsalted butter, softened

110 g caster sugar

500 g apricots, halved, stones removed, then quartered

3 cardamom pods, freshly ground

Warm the milk in a small saucepan over a low heat for 1–2 minutes. Transfer to the bowl of a stand mixer fitted with a dough hook and add the flour, yeast, salt, lemon zest, egg, butter and 50 g of the caster sugar. Mix on a medium speed for 4–5 minutes or until smooth and elastic. Transfer to a bowl lightly greased with butter, cover and stand in a warm place for 1 hour or until doubled in size.

Preheat the oven to 180°C. Line a 30 cm round tray with baking paper.

Tip the dough onto the tray using a pastry scraper then use your hands to press the dough out to the edge of the tray. Arrange the apricots on the dough in concentric circles, leaving a small border at the edge. Mix the remaining caster sugar with the cardamom and sprinkle over the apricots and any exposed dough.

Bake for 35 minutes or until the apricots are soft and the dough is risen and golden. Serve warm or on the day of baking.

To me, this is the most elegant way to end a dinner party – glistening poached peaches with sweet and delicate berries doused in velvety custard. Serve with *lingue di gatto* (cat's tongue) biscuits, which are buttery and sweet and can be dipped into the custard, as they do with zabaglione in Milan.

SUMMER FRUITS WITH VANILLA CUSTARD AND LINGUE DI GATTO

SERVES 6

6 yellow peaches

250 g caster sugar

1 vanilla pod, split and seeds scraped

100 ml marsala

raspberries or blackberries, to serve

LINGUE DI GATTO

100 g unsalted butter, softened

100 g icing sugar

1 vanilla pod, split and seeds scraped, or 1 teaspoon vanilla bean paste

100 g (⅔ cup) plain flour

100 g room-temperature egg whites (from 2–3 eggs)

pinch of fine sea salt

VANILLA CUSTARD

3 egg yolks

3 tablespoons caster sugar

1 tablespoon marsala

250 ml (1 cup) pure cream

200 ml full-cream milk

1 vanilla pod, split and seeds scraped, or 1 teaspoon vanilla bean paste

For the lingue di gatto, preheat the oven to 180°C and line two baking trays with baking paper. Cream the butter, icing sugar and vanilla together, either using a wooden spoon or a stand mixer fitted with a paddle attachment, until light and fluffy. Gently stir in the flour. In a separate and very clean bowl, whip the egg whites with a pinch of salt until you have stiff peaks. Gently fold the egg whites into the butter and sugar mixture, a little at a time, being careful not to knock out the air. Transfer the mixture to a piping bag fitted with a 10 mm plain nozzle. Pipe 5 cm lengths, leaving space for the biscuits to spread while cooking. Bake for 10 minutes or until the edges are lightly coloured. Transfer to a wire rack to cool, then store in an airtight container for up to a week. Makes about 30.

Using a small sharp knife, make a small cross in the base of each peach. Place the sugar, vanilla pod and seeds and the marsala in a large saucepan with 1 litre of water. Bring to the boil, then reduce to a gentle simmer. Carefully add the peaches, cover with a circle of baking paper and poach until tender but not too soft – you will be serving the peaches whole, so they should be cooked through but not falling apart. This can take anywhere between 10 and 20 minutes, depending on the size and ripeness of the peaches. Remove from the syrup and allow to cool. Carefully remove and discard the skin. Return the peaches to the cooled syrup and set aside in the fridge.

For the custard, whisk the egg yolks in a large bowl with the sugar and marsala until combined. Heat the milk with the vanilla in a medium saucepan over a low heat. Just before the milk comes to a simmer, take it off the heat and remove the vanilla pod. Slowly pour the hot milk into the egg mixture, whisking continuously. Pour the custard mixture into a clean saucepan over a low heat and cook, stirring continuously with a wooden spoon, for about 10 minutes until thickened. Keep warm if serving immediately, or store in the fridge with baking paper or plastic wrap placed directly on the custard to stop a skin forming.

Divide the peaches among serving bowls and spoon over some custard. Top with the berries and serve with the lingue di gatto biscuits for dipping.

Summer in Sicily is all about granita and brioche. For breakfast or a snack, this is the epitome of a summer treat. As the granita melts, the whipped cream and coffee turn into a sort of slush, and it is as glorious as you can imagine. Scoops of gelato are also commonly shovelled into sliced brioche, something that I highly recommend you try. This is one for summer holidays when there are no rules and granita with whipped cream and brioche is a very acceptable breakfast. If you can't find Manitoba flour, use any other strong flour. You may need to start the brioche the day before you want to eat it, if you want to let the dough prove overnight in the fridge.

COFFEE GRANITA WITH WHIPPED CREAM AND BRIOCHE

SERVES 8

2 tablespoons caster sugar

400 ml very strong espresso

juice of ½ lemon

250 ml (1 cup) pure cream

1 tablespoon icing sugar, sifted

finely grated zest of ½ lemon, plus extra to serve

BRIOCHE

150 ml full-cream milk

300 g tipo 00 flour, sifted

100 g Manitoba 0 flour (see page 12), sifted

7 g active dry yeast

80 g caster sugar

1 tablespoon honey

2 eggs

finely grated zest of 1 lemon

finely grated zest of 1 orange

1 vanilla pod, split and seeds scraped, or 1 teaspoon vanilla bean paste

1 teaspoon fine sea salt

100 g unsalted butter, softened

EGG WASH

1 egg yolk

1 tablespoon full-cream milk

Dissolve the sugar into the coffee and allow to cool. Stir in the lemon juice, pour the mixture into a shallow dish and place in the freezer. Every hour for the next 4 hours or so, use a fork to scrape the mixture, creating fluffy ice crystals. Once the granita has been frozen and fluffed it is ready to serve.

Meanwhile, to make the dough for the brioche, warm the milk in a small saucepan over a low heat for 1–2 minutes. The milk should be a little hotter than lukewarm, around 40°C. If it becomes too hot, allow to cool slightly before using. Place the flours, yeast, sugar, honey, eggs, lemon and orange zest, vanilla and warm milk in the bowl of a stand mixer fitted with a dough hook. Mix for 10 minutes on high speed. Add the salt and continue to mix for another 10 minutes. Add the butter one tablespoon at a time, mixing well after each addition, and continue to mix until the dough is smooth and elastic, usually another 10 minutes. Transfer to a bowl lightly greased with butter and cover. Leave to sit in a warm place for 2 hours or until doubled in size or, alternatively, cover and allow to rise slowly in the fridge for 8–12 hours. Bring the dough back to room temperature before beginning the next step if refrigerated.

Using a pastry scraper or your hands, tip the dough onto a clean work surface. Cut the dough into eight even-sized pieces and then cut a small piece (about a fifth) from each of those pieces of dough. Now you should have eight large pieces and eight small pieces. Form each of the larger pieces into a ball and place on a baking paper–lined baking tray, allowing plenty of space for them to expand. Roll the small pieces into balls and set aside. Press into the middle of each larger ball with your finger, almost touching the bottom. Combine the ingredients for the egg wash, then brush a little in and around the hole you just made. Place a small ball into each of the holes. Cover the brioche buns lightly with a clean tea towel or plastic wrap and allow to rise for another 2 hours in a warm space.

CONTINUED OVERLEAF →

Preheat the oven to 180°C.

Bake the brioche buns for 15–20 minutes, or until golden and cooked through. Transfer to a wire rack to cool.

Whip the cream with the icing sugar and lemon zest until you have soft billowy peaks. Serve the granita in glasses with a generous dollop of the lemon-scented whipped cream, a brioche bun and an extra sprinkle of lemon zest.

AUTUMN

Early autumn is perhaps my favourite time of the year – tomatoes, berries and stone fruit are still to be found, as they happily overlap with figs and plums. But there is a feeling of inevitability and melancholy as a season changes, too, and this could not be more true than in autumn. The reddening of leaves turns quickly to a noticeable crunch underfoot, which can leave one feeling wistful for the summer gone by. But soon my thoughts turn to pumpkins and crisp mornings, and I am ready to let go of the warmth of summer for another year.

Getting granola right is a tricky thing. You want it to be crunchy and clustery without being too sweet. This is our house granola. It can be sprinkled on yoghurt, served with milk, or with labneh and poached fruits as I've done here. The secret to good granola is cooking it low and slow and not disturbing it too much while in the oven. I let it cool completely before transferring to a jar or container. To make your own labneh, simply tie plain yoghurt in a clean muslin cloth and allow to hang over a bowl for at least 4 hours until thick and creamy.

GRANOLA WITH POACHED PLUMS

MAKES APPROXIMATELY 1 KG

300 g (3 cups) rolled oats

80 g (½ cup) hulled buckwheat

50 g (3¾ cups) puffed millet

55 g (1 cup) coconut flakes

2 tablespoons black sesame seeds

2 tablespoons white sesame seeds

100 g (¾ cup) pumpkin seeds

40 g (⅓ cup) sunflower seeds

155 g (1 cup) almonds

flaky sea salt

80 ml (⅓ cup) extra-virgin olive oil

100 ml maple syrup

175 g (½ cup) honey

2 tablespoons brown sugar

1 teaspoon ground cinnamon

1 vanilla pod, split and seeds scraped, or 1 teaspoon vanilla bean paste

¼ teaspoon baking powder

100 g dried fruit, such as apricots, sultanas, sour cherries etc.

labneh or milk, to serve

POACHED PLUMS

3 tablespoons marsala

2 tablespoons brown sugar

juice of ½ lemon

6 blood plums, halved and stones removed

Preheat the oven to 150°C. Line two large baking trays with baking paper.

In a large bowl, mix together the oats, buckwheat, millet, coconut, seeds, almonds and a large pinch of salt.

Meanwhile, combine the olive oil, maple syrup, honey, brown sugar, cinnamon, vanilla and 1 tablespoon of water in a medium saucepan and bring to a simmer over a medium heat, stirring to dissolve the sugar and honey. Stir in the baking powder and take off the heat – it should foam up. Immediately pour the hot mixture into the oats and stir so that everything is well coated.

Divide the mixture evenly over the prepared trays. It should sit relatively flat to ensure even cooking. If the trays are too crowded, use three trays instead. Bake for 1 hour or until a deep golden colour. During the cooking, stir the granola every 20 minutes, more often towards the end, to ensure it isn't burning and everything is cooking evenly. Allow to cool completely on the trays, then break up into clusters. Add the dried fruit and transfer to jars or an airtight container. The granola will keep in the pantry for up to 3 months.

For the poached plums, simply combine the marsala, brown sugar, lemon juice and 2 tablespoons of water in a small saucepan over a medium heat, stirring to dissolve the sugar. Add the plums and cover with a lid. Simmer for 5–10 minutes or until the plums have just collapsed. Allow to cool.

Serve the granola topped with the plums and a dollop of labneh or some milk.

This is my dream breakfast, which luckily we eat most weekends. Breakfast is a lovely ritual in our family and I really treasure slow mornings when we can sit and eat and forget the busyness of everyday life.

I always feel so nourished and warm after this meal and it's something that I make as simple or as elaborate as I want. Sometimes it's just the rice, miso soup and pickles, while other times, salmon and *tamagoyaki* (a rolled Japanese omelette) make it to the table, too. My husband, Nori, usually makes the omelette – he's faster and it's no trouble for him – but I have been practising and improving every time. If you don't have the special square or rectangular tamagoyaki pan, the mixture can be used to make scrambled eggs or a regular omelette instead. You will need to begin this recipe the night before to soak the mixed grains.

JAPANESE BREAKFAST

SERVES 4

MIXED-GRAIN RICE

110 g (½ cup) brown rice

110 g (about ½ cup) mixed grains, such as barley, chickpeas, black rice, millet, etc.

220 g (1 cup) white short-grain rice

MISO SOUP

10 g bonito flakes (katsuobushi)

60 g miso paste (any variety)

250 g soft tofu, cut into cubes

1 tablespoon wakame

2 spring onions, finely sliced

GRILLED SALMON

sea salt

2 x 150 g skin-on salmon fillets, halved lengthways

2 tablespoons olive oil or vegetable oil

TAMAGOYAKI

4 eggs

1 teaspoon caster sugar

1 tablespoon mirin

To make the mixed-grain rice, combine the brown rice and the mixed grains in a large bowl or container. Cover with cold water and soak overnight. Rinse, agitating the grains with your hands, and drain. Place in a large saucepan along with the white rice and cover with 810 ml (3¼ cups) of cold water. Bring to the boil over high heat, reduce the heat to medium and simmer for 5 minutes. Cover and reduce to low, cooking for a further 10 minutes. Try to avoid lifting the lid at this stage as you want to keep all the steam in. Allow the rice to sit, covered, for 15 minutes. Alternatively, cook in a rice cooker.

Meanwhile, for the miso soup, first make the dashi (stock). Bring 1 litre of water to the boil in a saucepan and add the bonito flakes. Reduce to a simmer and cook for 1 minute. Turn off the heat and allow to steep for 5 minutes. Strain the dashi into a larger saucepan, reserving the bonito flakes for another use (they can be stored in the fridge and used one more time to make dashi). Bring to a simmer over a medium–high heat and add the miso paste. This is traditionally done through a small coarse strainer called a miso koshi, which comes with a wooden pestle to break up any lumps as the miso goes into the soup. If you don't have one, press the miso through a fine-mesh sieve using the back of a spoon, then ladle some dashi through the strainer so you don't leave any miso behind. (Alternatively, mix some of the dashi into the miso or just break up any lumps before adding.) Add the tofu and wakame, turn off the heat and cover to keep warm while you prepare the rest of the breakfast.

For the salmon, generously salt the salmon. Heat the oil in a small frying pan over a medium heat and cook the salmon, skin-side down, for 2 minutes, followed by another minute on each side. Allow to rest.

For the tamagoyaki, whisk the eggs, sugar and mirin in a bowl. Heat a tamagoyaki pan over a low–medium heat and add enough egg mixture to cover the base of the pan in a thin layer. When the egg has cooked on the bottom but is still slightly wobbly on top, use chopsticks to roll up the omelette, starting from one short edge and rolling to the other short edge. Now you should have a rolled omelette at one end of a mostly empty pan. Pour in some more egg to cover the base of the pan and, once cooked, roll again, this time starting from the already-rolled omelette. Repeat until all of the egg mixture has been used. Transfer to a board and slice into roughly 2.5 cm thick pieces. Depending on how large your pan is, you may need to make two batches of omelette.

Divide the rice among four small bowls. Ladle the miso soup into four other bowls and sprinkle with the spring onion. Arrange the pieces of salmon and tamagoyaki on small plates and serve. We eat this breakfast with pickles and finish with a piece of orange, mandarin or grapefruit.

NOTES: I love mixed-grain rice; it's more substantial and provides interesting texture and nuttiness, depending on what grains you use. I tend to make a jar full of the uncooked grains and just store them in the pantry.

With the miso soup, the base is a simple dashi made from *katsuobushi* (dried bonito flakes). There are so many ways to make dashi – shiitake, kombu, chicken – it is simply a type of stock. Powdered dashi is available at Japanese grocers and if you don't want to make the soup from scratch, instant miso soup can usually be found in supermarkets now. Once you have all of the ingredients though, it is really little effort to make it from scratch.

I use a stovetop clay pot to cook rice at home, so exact cooking times may vary depending on the size and kind of pot you use. If in doubt, follow the packet directions or the instructions on your particular rice cooker.

Piadina or Piadina Romagnola is the most wonderful Italian flatbread coming specifically from the historical Romagna region, although versions are found all over Italy these days. Recipes don't vary all that much and are simply made with flour, some sort of fat, salt, water and sometimes milk. The most notable variation is in the diameter and thickness, which will change depending on where you are in the region. Traditionally cooked on a terracotta dish called a *teggia*, a regular frying pan works fine. I've suggested two autumnal fillings here, but the possibilities are endless – just keep it to three or four good-quality ingredients.

PIADINA WITH TWO FILLINGS

SERVES 8

500 g tipo 00 or plain flour, plus extra for dusting

2 teaspoons baking powder

1 teaspoon fine sea salt

80 g unsalted butter, softened

150 ml full-cream milk

150 ml lukewarm water

Combine the flour, baking powder and salt in a large bowl. Either using your hands or a stand mixer fitted with a dough hook, mix in the butter. Slowly pour in the milk and water and continue to mix until everything is well incorporated. If making the dough by hand, tip the dough onto a well-floured board and knead for around 10 minutes or until the dough is smooth and pliable. If using a stand mixer, mix on a medium speed for 5 minutes. Wrap the dough in plastic wrap and allow to rest for at least 30 minutes. I have had much success leaving it to rest in the fridge overnight, too. Just be sure to bring it back to room temperature before rolling.

Flour your work surface, divide the dough into eight balls and roll out into 2 mm thick rounds. Heat a large frying pan over a medium heat and cook the piadina for about 90 seconds on each side. Transfer to a plate and repeat with the remaining dough. Fill the piadina with your desired filling (see below) and enjoy. Piadina are best eaten shortly after being cooked.

Mozzarella, prosciutto, figs and rocket
Cover one half of the piadina with a few pieces of buffalo mozzarella and sliced fig. Drape over some prosciutto and top it all off with some basil leaves and rocket. Drizzle with extra-virgin olive oil and season with salt and pepper. Fold the piadina over, cut in half and serve.

Cime di rapa and stracciatella
Trim a bunch of cime di rapa (broccoli rabe) to remove any tough and woody stems. Blanch in salted boiling water until just wilted. Drain and refresh in iced water, then squeeze out as much moisture as you can. In a large frying pan, warm 2 tablespoons of extra-virgin olive oil. Add 3 roughly chopped garlic cloves and sauté gently until soft. Add a pinch of dried chilli flakes and the cime di rapa. Drag the rapa around the pan to coat. Season with salt and allow to cool briefly. Cover one half of the piadina with some cime di rapa and top with stracciatella (or mozzarella). Drizzle with olive oil, then fold the piadina over, cut in half and serve.

If you find yourself in Modena, chances are you will eat *gnocco fritto* (pillowy fried dough) at some point in the day. Whether for breakfast or as a snack with prosciutto, cheese or salami, they're incredible. They are really easy to eat – almost too easy – so I suggest having a small crowd at the ready to help you devour them. Traditionally fried in pork fat, I've opted for a neutral vegetable oil here.

GNOCCO FRITTO

SERVES 8–10 AS A SNACK

400 g tipo 00 flour,
plus extra for dusting

5 g active dry yeast

fine sea salt

50 g unsalted butter, softened

1 tablespoon olive oil

180–200 ml full-cream
milk, warmed

vegetable oil, for frying

thinly sliced prosciutto,
to serve

In a large bowl, combine the flour, yeast and a pinch of salt. Add the butter and, using your fingertips, rub it into the flour until the mixture resembles fine crumbs. Pour in the olive oil followed by the warm milk and incorporate using your hands until you have a soft, but not sticky, dough. Turn out the dough onto a floured work surface and knead for 5 minutes or until smooth. Cover and rest for 3–4 hours at room temperature.

Dust your work surface with flour and roll out the dough to a 3 mm thickness. Using a fluted pastry cutter or a knife, cut the dough into 4 cm squares. You can cut bigger squares if you like, however I do prefer them this size.

Heat 5 cm of vegetable oil in a heavy-based saucepan or deep-fryer to 180°C, or hot enough that a cube of bread dropped into the oil turns golden brown in 15 seconds. Fry the gnocco in batches for about 4 minutes until they are puffy and slightly golden, flipping halfway. When you initially put the gnocco in the oil, spoon some of the oil over them to encourage them to puff up and become bubbly. Drain on paper towel, then serve immediately with the prosciutto.

By about the beginning of May, I tend to accept that we are well and truly marching towards winter. Mornings are decidedly colder and knobbly pumpkins of all different sizes and colours begin to show up at the market. While I make risotto most of the year, this pumpkin one is a firm favourite. It's rich and creamy, and so vibrant – which makes a nice contrast to the gloomier weather. There are several important stages to making a good risotto: the gentle frying of *il soffritto* (the vegetables); the toasting of the rice, called *la tostatura*; and finally, *la mantecatura*, the final step – once the rice is al dente, take it off the heat and vigorously stir in some butter and parmesan until glossy. A good risotto should be *all'onda*, which translates to wavy and refers to how loose and fluid it should be. Of course, in between there is the adding of the wine and stock, which plays a crucial role, too. I prefer to use Carnaroli rice here, but any risotto rice will do – just buy the best quality you can afford.

PUMPKIN RISOTTO

SERVES 4–6

3 tablespoons extra-virgin olive oil, plus extra to serve

70 g unsalted butter

1 onion, finely chopped

400 g pumpkin, cut into 2 cm pieces

350 g Carnaroli or other risotto rice

125 ml (½ cup) dry white wine or white vermouth

1.5 litres vegetable or light chicken stock (see Note)

50 g (½ cup) grated parmesan, plus extra to serve

sea salt

mascarpone, to serve

Warm the olive oil and 20 g of the butter in a large heavy-based saucepan over a low heat and gently fry the onion for around 5 minutes until beginning to soften but not colour. Increase the heat to medium and add the pumpkin, cooking for around 10 minutes, stirring occasionally, until lightly coloured. Scatter the rice into the pan and cook for 2 minutes, stirring constantly, to toast the grains. Pour in the wine or vermouth and allow it to absorb into the rice. Once the liquid has almost disappeared, begin to add the stock, a ladle at a time, stirring constantly and waiting for the rice to absorb almost all of the liquid before adding another. Begin checking the rice for doneness at the 15-minute mark. Once the rice is al dente and not absorbing liquid as easily, add one more ladleful of stock along with the parmesan and remaining butter. Stir with some vigour, really working the butter and parmesan into the risotto, until it is all combined and glossy – it should be quite loose and not sticky at all.

Season to taste, then ladle onto plates and top with a spoonful of mascarpone, a last drizzle of olive oil and a little extra grated parmesan.

NOTE: I make a really quick and simple stock for my risotto. I place a halved onion, a few celery stalks, a carrot, a few peppercorns and a bay leaf into a stockpot, cover with cold water and let it simmer for just 30–40 minutes, then season with a little salt to taste.

In early autumn, when fresh beans are abundant and tomatoes are still around and very sweet, a quick pasta like this is perfect. It's one of my favourite combinations and is simple enough to throw together during the week without much forethought. Although canned or dried beans can be substituted here, it is well worth using fresh ones if they are available. Podding the beans is actually rather pleasant and meditative. The fresh beans are beautifully flecked, looking almost as if they have been painted. Even though this colouring disappears once cooked, it is lovely to appreciate their fleeting beauty.

BORLOTTI BEAN, TOMATO AND ROCKET PASTA

SERVES 4

300 g podded fresh borlotti beans (about 500 g unpodded; see Note)

4 garlic cloves, 1 peeled and left whole, 3 roughly chopped

1 fresh bay leaf

2 tablespoons extra-virgin olive oil, plus extra to serve

250 g cherry tomatoes, halved

sea salt

1 tablespoon pitted small black olives (I use taggiasche)

320 g dried short pasta, such as penne, rigatoni or farfalle

large handful of rocket, roughly chopped

handful of basil leaves

40 g parmesan, grated

Place the beans, whole garlic clove and bay leaf in a large saucepan and cover with water. Bring to the boil, then reduce the heat and and simmer for 30–40 minutes until very tender. Drain, discarding the garlic and bay leaf.

Meanwhile, warm the olive oil in a large frying pan over a low heat and gently sauté the chopped garlic, just for 30 seconds until aromatic. Add the cherry tomatoes along with a pinch of salt and cook until the tomatoes are beginning to soften and create a sauce. Add the cooked beans and the olives and stir to combine.

Meanwhile, cook the pasta in a large saucepan of salted boiling water for a few minutes less than directed on the packet instructions. Drain, reserving 250 ml (1 cup) of the cooking water. Tip the pasta into the sauce, along with the rocket and basil. Increase the heat to medium and add most of the cooking water. Stir so that everything is well coated and simmer for 1–2 minutes, or until the sauce has thickened and the pasta is al dente. If the sauce begins to look dry, add the remaining cooking water. Stir through the parmesan and serve with an extra drizzle of olive oil.

NOTE: If you can't find fresh borlotti beans, use 100 g dried beans, soaked overnight and drained, or 400 g canned cooked borlotti beans, drained and rinsed. Boil the soaked dried beans as you would the fresh ones, but if you are using canned beans, drain and rinse them before adding to the sauce in the second step.

Poaching is a beautiful way to cook fish quickly. This is such a flavourful dish and comes together without much effort at all. Serve this with crusty bread or creamy polenta and the meal is complete.

TOMATO-POACHED FISH WITH SAFFRON AND CHICKPEAS

pinch of saffron threads

250 ml (1 cup) hot water

1 tablespoon extra-virgin olive oil

20 g unsalted butter

3 garlic cloves, roughly chopped

sea salt

½ teaspoon dried chilli flakes

125 ml (½ cup) dry white wine

200 g canned whole peeled tomatoes

3 parsley sprigs, leaves picked and roughly chopped, stalks reserved

400 g canned chickpeas, drained and rinsed

600 g skinless fillets of firm white fish, such as coral trout, bream, cod or rockling, cut into 3 cm pieces

juice of 1 lemon

crusty bread or soft polenta, to serve

Place the saffron threads in a small bowl and cover with the hot water. Set aside to steep for 10 minutes.

Meanwhile, warm the olive oil and butter in a large frying pan over a low heat. Add the garlic, a pinch of salt and the chilli flakes and gently cook for 3 minutes. You don't want the garlic to colour. Increase the heat to medium and pour in the wine, allowing it to simmer for 1 minute. Add the tomatoes, breaking them up with the back of a wooden spoon, along with the parsley stalks, chickpeas and the saffron and water. Allow to simmer gently for 10 minutes or until slightly thickened. Add the fish and poach for around 5 minutes until just cooked through. Remove the parsley stalks and discard. Season to taste.

Scatter with the chopped parsley leaves and finish with a good squeeze of lemon juice. Serve with crusty bread or on a bed of creamy polenta.

This is a typical Maltese salad that I loved when I was younger. We would eat it with some tuna, crusty bread slathered in tomato paste and olive oil and a generous helping of olives and capers – and that was lunch or dinner. I'll often serve this salad with grilled fish like King George whiting or garfish, or as part of an antipasto spread. It keeps very well in the fridge so is great to make ahead.

MALTESE WHITE BEAN SALAD

SERVES 4 AS A SIDE

150 g dried cannellini or butter beans, soaked in water overnight, drained and rinsed

1 carrot, trimmed and halved

2 garlic cloves, bruised

2 fresh bay leaves

4 parsley sprigs, leaves picked and finely chopped, stalks reserved

1 small red onion, very finely diced

finely grated zest and juice of 1 lemon

3 tablespoons extra-virgin olive oil

1 tablespoon red wine vinegar

sea salt and black pepper

Place the beans in a large saucepan along with the carrot, garlic, bay leaves and parsley stalks. Cover with plenty of water. Place the pan over a high heat and bring to the boil. Reduce the heat to medium and simmer until the beans are tender. This can take anywhere from 30 minutes to 1½ hours, depending on the freshness of the beans. Drain, discarding the carrot, garlic, bay leaves and parsley stalks, and set aside to cool slightly.

While the beans are still warm, but not hot, tip them into a small mixing bowl and add the remaining ingredients. Stir to coat and season with salt and pepper. The salad will keep for several days in the fridge and is even better the next day. Just be sure to bring it to room temperature before eating.

The balance of salty, sweet, nutty and aromatic makes this dish a true classic. I've eaten many versions of this pasta, but my favourite was in Sicily when I was a teenager, eaten while I was waiting for the ferry to Malta. It was served on plastic plates at the port, absolutely nothing fancy about it. I recreated this recipe from my memory of that time.

SPAGHETTI WITH SARDINES, PINE NUTS AND SULTANAS

SERVES 4

pinch of saffron threads

100 ml hot water

3 tablespoons extra-virgin olive oil

1 small onion, finely diced

1 small fennel bulb, finely diced, fronds reserved and roughly chopped

sea salt

pinch of dried chilli flakes

3 anchovy fillets, chopped

50 g (⅓ cup) pine nuts, toasted

100 g sultanas

200 g fresh sardines, filleted, or 125 g good-quality canned sardines in extra-virgin olive oil, drained

1 tablespoon red wine vinegar

320 g dried spaghetti

CRUNCHY BREADCRUMBS

3 tablespoons extra-virgin olive oil

100 g (1¼ cups) fresh breadcrumbs (see Note page 33)

sea salt

For the breadcrumbs, heat the olive oil in a large frying pan over a medium heat. Add the breadcrumbs and cook until they are golden and crunchy, stirring constantly to stop them burning. Remove from the heat, season with salt and set aside to cool.

Place the saffron threads in a small bowl and cover with the hot water. Set aside to steep for 10 minutes.

Warm the olive oil in a large frying pan over a low–medium heat. Fry the onion and fennel bulb with a pinch of salt for around 15 minutes until soft. Add the chilli and anchovy and stir through. Scatter in the pine nuts and sultanas, pour in the saffron and water, then add the fresh sardines (if using canned sardines, add them later when you pour in the vinegar). Simmer for 1–2 minutes or until the sardines are just cooked through. Add the vinegar to the sauce, along with the canned sardines (if not using fresh). Break the fish into large pieces with a wooden spoon.

Meanwhile, cook the spaghetti in a saucepan of generously salted boiling water for a few minutes less than directed on the packet instructions. Drain and reserve 250 ml (1 cup) of the cooking water.

Increase the heat under the sauce to medium and add the spaghetti, tossing it through the sauce along with most of the cooking water. Cook for 1–2 minutes until the pasta is well coated and al dente. If the sauce begins to look dry, add the remaining cooking water. Stir through most of the fennel fronds and check for seasoning. Top with the crunchy breadcrumbs and the remaining fennel fronds.

More of a suggested combination of flavours than a recipe, this salad (sometimes without the cheese) is a weekly favourite that accompanies many of our meals. I love to use a really nice crumbly blue cheese – it needs to have some body, so I tend to avoid creamy soft types.

RADICCHIO AND PEAR SALAD WITH BLUE CHEESE AND WALNUTS

SERVES 4

½ head of radicchio, leaves torn

3 celery stalks, preferably the younger inner heart, finely sliced

1 pear, quartered, cored and finely sliced

50 g (½ cup) walnuts, toasted and roughly chopped

80 g blue cheese, such as Stilton, Roquefort or Gorgonzola

DRESSING

2 tablespoons walnut or extra-virgin olive oil

juice of 1 lemon

1 very small garlic clove, finely grated

1 teaspoon dijon mustard

sea salt and black pepper

Simply arrange the radicchio, celery and pear on a serving plate. Scatter over the walnuts and crumble over the cheese.

Whisk the dressing ingredients together in a small bowl, then pour over the salad and serve.

I usually buy pumpkins whole; not only do they last better this way, they look beautiful and really bring autumn into the house. This salad is incredibly simple, but the roasted chillies make it a little special and add a lovely sweetness. I often add a few spoonfuls of ricotta to the salad and serve it with crusty bread for a complete meal.

ROASTED PUMPKIN, ROCKET AND BORLOTTI BEAN SALAD

SERVES 4

¼ kent pumpkin (about 850 g), cut into 3 cm wedges

3 long red chillies, halved lengthways and deseeded

3 tablespoons extra-virgin olive oil

sea salt

400 g canned borlotti beans, drained and rinsed (see Note)

handful of parsley leaves, roughly chopped

45 g (¼ cup) semi-dried pitted black olives

large handful of rocket

DRESSING

3 tablespoons extra-virgin olive oil

2 tablespoons red wine vinegar

finely grated zest of ½ lemon

1 small garlic clove, finely chopped or grated

sea salt

Preheat the oven to 180°C. Line a baking tray with baking paper.

Arrange the pumpkin wedges and chillies on the prepared tray. Drizzle with the olive oil and season generously with salt. Roast for 30–40 minutes or until the pumpkin is tender and caramelised and the chilli skin has blistered and the flesh softened.

Transfer the chillies to a small bowl and allow the pumpkin to cool on the tray.

While still warm, peel the skins from the chillies and discard, setting the flesh aside until you are ready to assemble the salad.

Arrange the cooled pumpkin wedges on a serving plate with the borlotti beans, roasted chillies, parsley, olives and rocket.

For the dressing, whisk the ingredients together in a small bowl. Drizzle over the salad and serve.

NOTE: Fresh borlotti beans are wonderful in this salad if they're available. Use 100 g podded fresh beans or, alternatively, you could also use 80 g dried borlotti beans (soak them overnight in cold water, then drain). Before adding to the salad, pop the fresh or soaked beans in a saucepan of water with a garlic clove and a bay leaf and simmer for 30–40 minutes until very tender. Drain, discarding the garlic and bay leaf.

Named by my four year old, these 'best fried potatoes' really are the best for a few reasons. Firstly, the soft fluffy potatoes with a crunchy ragged exterior; secondly, the herby, salty, zingy topping; and thirdly, they don't require long roasting in the oven. I choose small waxy potatoes for this recipe, as they are better eating and tend to hold their shape.

BEST FRIED POTATOES

SERVES 4

700 g small pink eye or any other waxy baby potatoes

1 tablespoon salted capers, rinsed

small handful of parsley leaves

1 small garlic clove

finely grated zest of 1 lemon

3 tablespoons extra-virgin olive oil

grated parmesan, to serve (optional)

Place the potatoes in a large saucepan of salted water and bring to the boil over a high heat. Cook for 25–30 minutes until the potatoes are tender, but not falling apart. Drain and set aside.

Meanwhile, roughly chop the capers on a board, then add the parsley and continue chopping. Now add the garlic and continue to chop until you have an almost paste-like mixture. Transfer to a bowl and add the lemon zest. Set aside.

Place the potatoes on a flat surface and, using something flat, such as a plate or the bottom of a pan, gently squash the potatoes. Don't completely crush them, you want them to mostly hold their shape.

Heat the olive oil in a large frying pan over a medium heat, add the potatoes and fry for around 10 minutes, stirring occasionally, until golden and crunchy. Scatter over the parsley mixture and gently move the potatoes around so they are coated and the capers become a little crispy. Serve with a generous grating of parmesan, if desired.

A warming bowl of curry is a welcome reprieve after a busy day. While I didn't grow up eating curries, I now crave them, in all of their different incarnations. This one is very straightforward and can be adapted to suit your tastes: pumpkin instead of sweet potato, black beans instead of chickpeas, not to mention varying the spices and aromatics. I make the paste using my mortar and pestle, which really isn't much more effort than a food processor (and I really don't enjoy cleaning a food processor). Choose a mortar and pestle that are large and heavy. Mine are marble, which makes the job easier. We eat this curry with thick homemade flatbread, which is incredibly simple to make.

SWEET POTATO AND SPINACH CURRY

SERVES 4

2 tablespoons extra-virgin olive oil

2 x 400 ml cans coconut cream

60 g roasted peanuts, finely crushed

750 g sweet potato, peeled and cut into large pieces

large handful of baby spinach leaves

400 g canned chickpeas or black beans

FLATBREAD

500 g (3⅓ cups) plain flour, plus extra for dusting (bread, tipo 0 or tipo 00 flours all work well for this, too)

5 g sea salt

6 g active dry yeast

1 tablespoon extra-virgin olive oil

280 ml warm water

CONTINUED OVERLEAF →

To make the dough for the flatbread, place the flour, salt, yeast and olive oil in the bowl of a stand mixer fitted with a dough hook. With the mixer on low, slowly pour in the warm water. Increase the mixer to medium, adding another tablespoon of water if there are still dry parts. Increase the mixer to high and knead for 5 minutes. The dough should be soft and just a little sticky. You can make the dough by hand, but you may need to add a little extra flour (resulting in slightly less soft flatbread). Transfer the dough to a large, lightly oiled bowl. Cover and allow to prove in a warm place for 1 hour or until doubled in size.

Tip the dough onto a lightly floured work surface using a pastry scraper or your hands. Divide the dough into eight pieces and shape each one into a smooth ball. I do this by slightly flattening each piece then folding the edges into the centre. Turn over so that the seam is at the bottom and, using the edges of your hands, turn the ball clockwise to create a smooth, tight surface. Cover and allow to prove for a further 45 minutes.

For the curry paste, pound the garlic, onion and ginger with a large pinch of salt using a mortar and pestle. Add the coriander stalks and root and continue to pound, then add the seeds and turmeric. Keeping pounding until you have a fairly smooth paste. Alternatively, blitz everything together in a food processor.

Heat the olive oil in a large heavy-based saucepan over a medium–high heat. Add the curry paste and fry, stirring constantly, for 2 minutes until fragrant and beginning to colour. Add the coconut cream and bring to a simmer. Reduce the heat to low and simmer for 5 minutes. Add the crushed peanuts followed by the sweet potato and simmer for 10–15 minutes until tender.

Meanwhile, roll out each dough ball to a 10 cm circle, around 8 mm thick. Heat a large frying pan over a high heat and cook the flatbread for 1 minute on each side or until cooked through. They should puff up as soon as they touch the pan and have golden spots on the surface. Immediately wrap the hot flatbread in a tea towel to steam and remain soft and pliable.

Stir the spinach and chickpeas or black beans into the curry and cook for a few minutes longer so the spinach is just wilted and the chickpeas or beans have warmed through. Season well, then divide among bowls and top with the coriander leaves and some onion or shallot, chilli, peanuts and a squeeze of lime juice. Serve the warm flatbread on the side.

CURRY PASTE

4 garlic cloves, chopped

1 onion, chopped

4 cm piece of ginger

sea salt

1 bunch of coriander, stalks
and roots washed and finely
chopped, leaves reserved
to serve

1 heaped teaspoon toasted
cumin seeds

1 heaped teaspoon toasted
coriander seeds

1 teaspoon mustard seeds

1 teaspoon ground turmeric

TO SERVE

sliced red onion or shallot

finely sliced green chilli

roasted peanuts

lime wedges

A comforting soup to welcome the change of season, but with a nod to summer just gone by in the way of crispy eggplant. It makes a lovely contrast to the creaminess of the soup.

SPICED SPLIT LENTIL SOUP WITH FRIED EGGPLANT

SERVES 4–6

3 tablespoons extra-virgin olive oil
1 onion, roughly chopped
2 carrots, roughly chopped
sea salt
4 garlic cloves, roughly chopped
3 cm piece of ginger, finely chopped
1 tablespoon cumin seeds, toasted and roughly ground
1 tablespoon coriander seeds, toasted and roughly ground
1 teaspoon ground ginger
1 teaspoon yellow mustard seeds
½ teaspoon dried chilli flakes
200 g red split lentils, washed
200 g canned whole peeled tomatoes
1 litre chicken stock
juice of 1 lemon

FRIED EGGPLANT

2 tablespoons plain flour
1 teaspoon ground cumin
pinch of sea salt
1 small eggplant (about 200 g), cut into 1.5 cm cubes
vegetable oil, for shallow-frying

TO SERVE

plain full-fat yoghurt
coriander leaves
roughly chopped toasted walnuts
lemon wedges
extra-virgin olive oil

Warm the olive oil in a large heavy-based saucepan over a low heat. Add the onion, carrot and a pinch of salt and cook for 10–15 minutes until the onion has softened and is just beginning to colour. Increase the heat to medium. Add the garlic, ginger and spices and cook for around 2 minutes until the spices are fragrant. Add the lentils and stir to coat them in all of the spices and aromatics. Pour in the tomatoes and chicken stock and simmer for 45 minutes or until the lentils are soft, stirring occasionally to stop them catching. Squeeze in the lemon juice, then, using a hand-held blender, roughly puree the soup.

Meanwhile, for the eggplant, combine the flour, cumin and salt in a small bowl. Toss the eggplant in the seasoned flour and shake off any excess. Heat 2 cm of oil in a small saucepan or frying pan over a medium heat and fry the eggplant in batches until golden and soft on the inside. Remove with a slotted spoon and drain on paper towel.

Ladle the soup into bowls, top with some yoghurt, the fried eggplant and some coriander, walnuts, a squeeze of lemon and a drizzle of olive oil.

Lamb cutlets are tender and juicy and the perfect cut for crumbing – by the time the outside is nice and crunchy, the interior has cooked to perfection. They pair so well with the smokiness of the eggplant, which is packed full of herbs and pomegranate.

CRUMBED LAMB CUTLETS WITH SMOKY EGGPLANT SALAD

SERVES 4

8 frenched lamb cutlets

sea salt

100 g (⅔ cup) plain flour

2 eggs, lightly beaten

150 g (2½ cups) panko or other white breadcrumbs

1 tablespoon extra-virgin olive oil

SMOKY EGGPLANT SALAD

3 eggplants (about 1 kg in total)

seeds of 1 pomegranate

60 g pine nuts, toasted

large handful of parsley leaves

large handful of mint leaves

juice of 1 lemon

3 tablespoons extra-virgin olive oil

1 tablespoon pomegranate molasses

pinch of sumac

For the salad, place the eggplants directly over the gas flame of your stove or on a barbecue over coals and cook for around 10 minutes, turning frequently, until the skin is charred and the flesh is soft and collapsed. Transfer to a dish and, when cool enough to handle, peel the skin off and discard. Transfer the flesh to a colander and allow to drain for 10 minutes. Transfer to a bowl and add the remaining ingredients, using a fork to gently pull the eggplant apart as you mix it with the other ingredients.

Season the lamb with salt. Place the flour, egg and breadcrumbs in separate shallow bowls ready for crumbing. First, lightly dust the cutlets in flour, then dip in the egg and finish with the breadcrumbs, using your hands to gently press the crumbs on.

Heat the olive oil in a large frying pan over a medium heat and pan-fry the crumbed lamb cutlets for about 3 minutes on each side, until golden and just cooked through. Drain on paper towel, then serve with the eggplant salad.

Inspired by a Maltese pumpkin and rice pie, this version is super fresh with lots of herbs, spices and lemon. The raisins add a lovely sweetness and the pine nuts give some texture to the filling. The pastry is very simple to make and can be prepared ahead of time, as can the filling. In fact, the whole pie can be assembled the day before and kept uncooked, covered in the fridge. Just save the egg wash until just before it goes in the oven. I like to use kent pumpkin, but butternut is my second choice as it's very versatile and has great texture.

PUMPKIN PIE

SERVES 4–6

500 g (3⅓ cups) plain flour

pinch of fine sea salt

250 g chilled unsalted butter, cut into cubes

1 tablespoon white vinegar

100–150 ml iced water

1 egg, lightly beaten

PUMPKIN AND RICE FILLING

1 kg kent or butternut pumpkin, cut into large chunks with the skin left on

100 ml extra-virgin olive oil

sea salt

1 teaspoon mixed spice

½ teaspoon ground cinnamon

100 g short-grain brown rice

1 onion, finely diced

3 garlic cloves, finely chopped

50 g (⅓ cup) pine nuts, toasted

60 g (½ cup) raisins

1 roma tomato, roughly chopped

large handful of mint leaves, roughly chopped

large handful of parsley leaves, roughly chopped

finely grated zest of 1 lemon

sea salt and black pepper

Tip the flour onto a clean work surface and sprinkle with the salt. Add the butter and toss so that all the pieces are coated. Rub the butter into the flour using your fingertips, until you have a mixture that's the consistency of coarse breadcrumbs. Try to leave some larger pieces, as this will create a flaky crust during baking. Sprinkle over the vinegar, then pour over the water – just a little at a time, as you may not need it all and it is much easier to add more as you go than to have too much in the beginning. Bring the flour and butter together with your hands to form a dough with no dry crumbs left. Divide into two, flatten into rounds and cover with plastic wrap. Chill in the fridge for around 30 minutes.

Preheat the oven to 180°C. Line a baking tray with baking paper.

For the filling, arrange the pumpkin on the prepared tray, skin-side down. Drizzle with half of the olive oil and scatter with salt and the spices. Roast for around 35 minutes until tender. Set aside to cool, then scoop the flesh into a large bowl, discarding the skin.

Cook the rice according to the packet instructions until tender, then drain and add to the pumpkin. Meanwhile, heat the remaining olive oil in a large frying pan over a low heat and cook the onion with a pinch of salt for 10–15 minutes until soft and just beginning to colour. Add the garlic and cook for a further 1 minute until fragrant. Add the onion mixture to the pumpkin and allow to cool. Stir in the remaining ingredients and season well.

CONTINUED OVERLEAF →

Line a 20 cm round baking tray with baking paper.

Remove the pastry dough from the fridge 5 minutes before you are ready to use it, as this will make it easier to roll. On a floured work surface, roll out one of the pastry pieces into a 24 cm circle about 2.5 mm thick. Drape the pasty over the tray – there should be about 2 cm of overhanging pastry. Roll out the second piece of dough to the same size. Spoon the pumpkin filling over the pastry base, spreading it all the way to the edge. Drape the second piece of pastry over the filling and trim both layers of pastry so that there is only 1 cm of overhanging pastry. Press the pastry together, folding and crimping the pie to seal it all in. It should now be sitting snugly within the tray. Whisk 1 teaspoon of water into the egg to make a wash. Make a cut in the centre of the pie to allow steam to escape and brush the pie with the egg wash.

Bake for 35–40 minutes until the pie has puffed up and the pastry is golden.

Known as *Torta Pasqualina*, this pie is so substantial and satisfying both to make and to eat. The pastry is rather unusual and requires you to make several thin sheets of dough, which are layered to create an almost filo-type pastry. Once the filling has been spooned into the base, deep holes are made where eggs are nestled. Once cooked, the eggs are dramatic and visually very beautiful next to the green filling. If you don't want to make the pastry (but I urge you to try) store-bought filo would work well, as would shortcrust. This pie is best served hot from the oven.

SILVERBEET AND RICOTTA EASTER PIE

SERVES 6–8

400 g tipo 00 flour, plus extra for dusting

pinch of fine sea salt

2 tablespoons extra-virgin olive oil, plus extra for brushing

200 ml iced water

5 eggs

SILVERBEET AND RICOTTA FILLING

300 g fresh full-fat ricotta

50 g parmesan, grated

pinch of freshly grated nutmeg

finely grated zest of 1 lemon

2 tablespoons extra-virgin olive oil

1 onion, finely sliced

sea salt

3 garlic cloves, finely chopped

800 g silverbeet leaves, washed and finely chopped

iced water, for refreshing

800 g English spinach leaves, washed and finely chopped

2 teaspoons oregano or marjoram leaves, finely chopped

2 eggs, lightly beaten

Preheat the oven to 180°C. Grease a 23 cm round springform tin with olive oil.

Combine the flour and salt in a large bowl. Pour in the olive oil and water and mix with your hands until the mixture forms a ball. Tip the dough onto a floured work surface and knead for 5 minutes or until smooth. Divide the dough into six balls and cover with a clean tea towel.

For the filling, combine the ricotta, parmesan, nutmeg and lemon zest in a bowl. Heat the olive oil in a frying pan over a low–medium heat and gently fry the onion with a pinch of salt for 10 minutes until soft. Add the garlic and cook for a minute longer. Set aside to cool. Blanch the silverbeet in a large saucepan of salted boiling water until wilted, refresh in iced water and drain, squeezing out as much liquid as possible. Repeat this process with the spinach and add both greens to the ricotta along with the cooled onion mixture and the oregano or marjoram. Add the egg and gently stir until well combined.

On a lightly floured work surface, roll out one of the balls of dough to a very thin circle, as thin as you can roll it, stretching with your hands to help it along. Drape the pastry into the prepared tin and brush with olive oil. Roll out the next two balls of dough, repeating the draping and brushing. There should be about 4 cm of dough overhanging the tin.

Spoon the filling into the tin and spread to level the mixture. Using the back of a spoon, make four deep indentations in the mixture and crack an egg into each of them. Repeat the rolling, draping and brushing with the three remaining balls of dough to make a top for your pie. Trim the overhanging pastry to just 2 cm, then fold in the dough edge, crimping as you go, to seal the pie. Whisk 1 teaspoon of water into the remaining egg to make a wash and brush the top of the pie and the crimped edge. Using a small sharp knife, poke a few steam holes in the middle of the pie.

Bake for 45–50 minutes until the pastry is golden and the pie is piping hot in the middle. Check by inserting a metal skewer into the pie; it should come out very hot to the touch. Allow to cool briefly, then remove the pie from the tin and transfer to a serving plate or board. Serve hot.

I have a real love for udon noodles – they're so comforting. It must have something to do with their thickness, I think. I never tire of eating them in different ways. In Tokyo, for breakfast, served in broth with tempura; topped with many slices of *sudachi* – a small green citrus fruit with a very sour flavour; or eaten cold with a dipping sauce. At home, though, I usually make them like this: fried with pork mince, wombok and shiitake, all topped with a spicy chilli oil.

SPICY PORK AND SHIITAKE UDON NOODLES

SERVES 4

3 tablespoons extra-virgin olive oil

500 g pork mince

4 garlic cloves, roughly chopped

2 cm piece of ginger, finely chopped

2 spring onions, finely chopped, plus extra, sliced, to serve

100 g fresh shiitake mushrooms, sliced

½ wombok (about 500 g), finely sliced

80 ml (⅓ cup) light soy sauce

80 ml (⅓ cup) mirin

80 ml (⅓ cup) saké

1 teaspoon caster sugar

400 g dried udon noodles

toasted white and black sesame seeds, to serve

sesame oil, to serve

CHILLI OIL

200 ml vegetable oil

4 garlic cloves, finely chopped

2 cm piece of ginger, finely chopped

2 spring onions, finely sliced

2 tablespoons dried chilli flakes

1 teaspoon hot chilli powder

1 tablespoon sesame seeds

1 teaspoon sea salt

For the chilli oil, heat the oil in a small saucepan over a medium heat. Add the remaining ingredients and fry for 1–2 minutes or until fragrant and golden. Transfer to a jar and allow to cool before using.

Heat half of the olive oil in a large frying pan or wok over a high heat and brown the mince, breaking up any lumps with the back of a wooden spoon. Transfer to a bowl and reduce the heat to medium. Pour in the remaining olive oil and fry the garlic, ginger, spring onion and mushroom for 3 minutes until fragrant and beginning to soften. Add the wombok and cook everything for a further 2 minutes or until the wombok has begun to wilt. Return the mince to the pan or wok and add the soy, mirin, saké and sugar, stirring well to combine. Simmer until the sauce has reduced slightly and the cabbage is cooked, but not soft.

Meanwhile, cook the noodles according to the packet instructions. Drain and add to the pan or wok, tossing so that the noodles are well coated. Spoon into bowls and top with extra spring onion, a scattering of sesame seeds and a small drizzle of sesame oil. Spoon some of the chilli oil on top of each bowl and serve.

Miso paste is such an effortless way to add flavour to chicken. When combined with the other ingredients, the miso creates a well-rounded marinade that caramelises once in the oven. When I first made this, my husband, Nori, said it tasted like something his father used to make when he was younger, and it has since become a firm favourite in our home. I serve it with a crisp nashi and wombok salad and some steamed rice, too, if I'm after a more filling meal.

MISO ROAST CHICKEN

SERVES 4–6

1 kg chicken thighs, skin on

60 g red miso paste

3 tablespoons light soy sauce, plus extra if needed

3 tablespoons saké

3 tablespoons mirin

2 garlic cloves, grated

2 cm piece of ginger, grated

pinch of caster sugar, plus extra if needed

NASHI AND CABBAGE SALAD

350 g wombok, finely sliced

1 red shallot, finely sliced

2 spring onions, finely sliced

1 large nashi (about 250 g), quartered, cored and finely sliced

large handful of mint leaves, roughly chopped

2 tablespoons grapeseed oil

1 tablespoon sesame oil

2 tablespoons rice wine vinegar

1 tablespoon light soy sauce

1 tablespoon toasted sesame seeds

pinch of sea salt

Place the chicken in a large non-reactive bowl. In a small bowl, whisk the miso, soy, saké, mirin, garlic, ginger and sugar together until smooth. Check for seasoning, balancing with more soy or sugar if needed. Pour over the chicken and mix well, ensuring the chicken is well coated. Cover and marinate in the fridge for at least 1 hour, but preferably 4 hours.

Preheat the oven to 180°C.

Arrange the marinated chicken, skin-side up, in a single layer in a shallow baking tray. Any excess marinade can be poured over the chicken. Roast for 35 minutes or until the chicken is just cooked through and the skin is golden and slightly burnished. If the chicken hasn't coloured as much as desired, increase the temperature to 200°C in the last 5 minutes.

Meanwhile, for the salad, place the wombok, shallot, spring onion, nashi and mint in a large bowl. Whisk the oils, vinegar, soy, sesame seeds and salt together. Pour over the salad and toss well to combine. Serve alongside the chicken.

Ricotta is something I always have in my fridge. I love it on toast in the mornings or dolloped over pasta. It's also wonderful in desserts, and nothing showcases ricotta in quite the same way as this tart. Studded with Italian candied citrus and dark chocolate, it's inspired by the *Pastiera* – a Neapolitan tart traditionally eaten at Easter time.

SWEET RICOTTA TART

SERVES 8

700 g fresh full-fat ricotta

100 g caster sugar

200 ml pure cream

finely grated zest of 1 lemon

1 tablespoon marsala

1 vanilla pod, split and seeds scraped, or 1 teaspoon vanilla extract

2 eggs, plus 1 egg yolk, lightly beaten

50 g dark chocolate (70% cocoa), finely chopped

2–3 tablespoons finely chopped Italian candied fruit (see Note)

3 tablespoons pine nuts

SWEET PASTRY

300 g (2 cups) plain flour, plus extra for dusting

150 g chilled unsalted butter, cut into cubes

80 g (⅓ cup) caster sugar

1 egg, plus 1 egg yolk

finely grated zest of 1 lemon

1 vanilla pod, split and seeds scraped, or 1 teaspoon vanilla extract

To make the dough for the pastry, pulse the flour and butter together in a food processor until you have pea-sized lumps of butter. Add the sugar and pulse to combine. Add the egg and yolk, lemon zest and vanilla and continue to pulse until the mixture almost forms a ball. Tip the dough onto a work surface and bring it together with your hands. Wrap in plastic wrap and flatten into a disc. Refrigerate for at least 1 hour.

Preheat the oven to 180°C.

On a lightly floured work surface, roll out the pastry to a 2 mm thickness. Drape into a deep 24 cm fluted tart tin, pressing the pastry into the tin. Roll your rolling pin along the edges of the tin to trim any excess pastry, then refrigerate for 15 minutes.

Meanwhile, whisk the ricotta, sugar and cream together in a large bowl until smooth. Change to a wooden spoon and stir in the lemon zest, marsala and vanilla. Gently stir in the egg until just combined, followed by the chocolate and candied fruit. Pour into the chilled pastry case, then top with the pine nuts.

Bake for 30–35 minutes until the pastry is golden and the filling is just set – it should still be a little wobbly. Allow to cool, then refrigerate for at least 2 hours until chilled. Remove from the tin and serve.

NOTE: Italian candied fruits, most commonly cedro (a type of citrus), pear, fig and mandarin, can be found at Italian delis and grocers. They are used in a range of Italian desserts, including cannoli, cassata and sweet breads like panettone. If unavailable and you can't find a good-quality substitute, just leave them out – the tart will still be lovely.

While pavlovas get a good look in during summer, an autumnal pavlova is a wonderful way to show off fruit like figs and plums. The contrast in colours is beautiful. Of course, this can be made any time of the year and just adapted to what fruits are in season: mangoes and lychees in summer, poached rhubarb in spring and citrus in winter. I've made individual pavlovas here – they make a rather elegant dessert, but this recipe works just as well as a larger single pavlova. Ideally, you should start the meringues the day before you wish to serve them to allow for cooling.

PAVLOVAS WITH FIGS, PLUMS AND ALMONDS

SERVES 6

5 egg whites

pinch of fine sea salt

250 g caster sugar

1 tablespoon cornflour, sifted

2 teaspoons white vinegar

45 g (½ cup) flaked almonds, roughly chopped

200 ml pure cream

200 g crème fraîche

1 teaspoon rosewater

TO SERVE

sliced figs

sliced plums

toasted flaked almonds

Preheat the oven to 120°C and line a large baking tray with baking paper.

Place the egg whites and salt in the bowl of a stand mixer fitted with a whisk attachment and beat until soft peaks form. Gradually add the sugar, 1 tablespoon at a time, until the mixture is stiff and glossy and all the sugar has dissolved. It is really important that there aren't any sugar granules in the meringue, so take a little of the mixture and rub it between two fingers to check. Continue to beat if it hasn't completely dissolved, then check again. Gently stir in the cornflour, vinegar and almonds.

Make six round mounds of meringue on the prepared tray, keeping the sides high and creating a slight dip in the middle.

Bake for approximately 1 hour. The meringue should be crisp on the outside, but not coloured. Switch off the oven and open the door slightly, then leave the meringues in there to cool for at least 4 hours, preferably overnight.

Carefully transfer the cooled meringues to a serving dish or tray. If you're not using them immediately, store in an airtight container at room temperature for up to 4 days.

Meanwhile, whip the cream and crème fraîche using the electric mixer until soft peaks form. Add the rosewater and continue to whip until the mixture is just becoming stiff, being careful not to over-whip. You want soft billowy mounds of cream.

Pile the cream onto each meringue shell and top with slices of fresh fig or plum and some flaked almonds. Serve immediately.

This recipe is inspired by the carrot cake my mum would make when I was younger. Vary the spices and nuts to suit, but, whatever you do, do not skip the cream cheese frosting. I use extra-virgin olive oil in this recipe, but regular olive oil or a neutral vegetable oil will work well, too.

SPICED CARROT CAKE

SERVES 8–10

380 g (2½ cups) plain flour

1½ teaspoons baking powder

1 tablespoon ground cinnamon

½ teaspoon freshly grated nutmeg

½ teaspoon ground cardamom (ideally freshly ground)

4 eggs

150 g (⅔ cup, firmly packed) brown sugar

150 g (⅔ cup) caster sugar

200 ml extra-virgin olive oil

4 carrots (about 375 g in total), coarsely grated

100 g walnuts or shelled pistachios, roughly chopped (optional), plus extra for topping

coconut flakes, for topping

CREAM CHEESE FROSTING

150 g icing sugar, sifted

100 g unsalted butter, softened

250 g cream cheese, softened

finely grated zest of 1 lime

pinch of ground cinnamon

Preheat the oven to 170°C. Grease a 22 cm round cake tin with butter and line with baking paper.

Sift the flour, baking powder and cinnamon into a large bowl and add the nutmeg and cardamom.

In a separate large bowl, beat the eggs together with the sugars and olive oil until light and pale. This easiest done using a stand mixer fitted with a whisk attachment, but by hand is fine, too. Gently fold in the dry ingredients, then add the carrot and chopped nuts (if using). Spoon into the prepared tin and bake for 1 hour or until a skewer comes out clean when inserted in the centre.

Leave to cool in the tin for 10 minutes, then invert onto a wire rack to cool completely.

Meanwhile, for the frosting, place the icing sugar and butter in the bowl of a stand mixer fitted with a whisk attachment and beat for around 4 minutes until smooth, pale and fluffy. Now beat in the cream cheese until smooth and aerated. Gently stir in the lime zest and cinnamon – I do this by hand with a spatula to avoid the zest getting caught in the whisk. Spread over the cooled cake and top with nuts and coconut flakes.

I took this to a picnic in early autumn when the warmth of the sun was noticeable and sitting outside to eat dinner was still pleasant. The pudding was still warm from the oven and was perfect with double cream. Almost like a crumble, but with a spongy cake on top instead, it is really comforting and would see you well into winter by using frozen berries.

BLACKBERRY AND APPLE PUDDING

SERVES 4–6

3 granny smith apples (about 650 g in total) peeled, cored and cut into 5 mm thick slices

finely grated zest and juice of 1 lemon

2 teaspoons vanilla extract

150 g raw sugar

250 g fresh or frozen and thawed blackberries

100 g unsalted butter, softened

2 eggs, lightly beaten

3 tablespoons full-cream milk

150 g (1 cup) self-raising flour, sifted

double cream, to serve

CINNAMON SUGAR TOPPING

1 tablespoon raw sugar

1 teaspoon ground cinnamon

1 tablespoon melted unsalted butter

Preheat the oven to 170°C. Grease a 28 cm round baking dish with butter.

Combine the apple in a large bowl with the lemon juice, half the vanilla and 50 g of the sugar. Toss so that everything is well coated. Gently stir through the blackberries, then tumble the fruit into the prepared baking dish.

Cream the butter with the remaining sugar in a large bowl until pale and fluffy. Add the remaining vanilla and the eggs, mixing well until everything is well incorporated. Stir in the milk. It may look curdled at this stage, but it will come together. Finally, add the lemon zest and flour and gently mix until the batter is smooth. Spread the batter over the top of the fruit, smoothing the top with a spatula. Bake for 35–40 minutes or until the top springs back when touched.

Meanwhile, for the topping, combine the sugar and cinnamon in a small bowl. Brush the hot pudding with melted butter and scatter over the cinnamon sugar. Serve warm with double cream.

A classic and simple chocolate cake recipe that I know by heart, perhaps because I want to be able to whip it up whenever I need to, but also because it really is so simple. I like cakes baked in loaf tins – they remind me of Parisian bakeries and the ones in Tokyo alike. Simply dusted with more cocoa, this is a real crowd-pleaser.

DOUBLE CHOCOLATE LOAF

SERVES 8

150 g (1 cup) self-raising flour

30 g unsweetened Dutch-process cocoa powder, plus extra for dusting

pinch of fine sea salt

150 g unsalted butter, softened

200 g brown sugar

1 vanilla pod, split and seeds scraped, or 1 teaspoon vanilla bean paste

2 eggs

150 g dark chocolate (70% cocoa), melted and cooled

150 ml hot coffee or water

Preheat the oven to 180°C. Grease a 23 cm loaf tin with butter and line with baking paper or dust with cocoa powder.

Sift the flour, cocoa powder and salt into a small bowl and set aside.

Cream the butter, sugar and vanilla together, either using a wooden spoon or a stand mixer fitted with a paddle attachment, until pale and fluffy. Add one egg at a time, beating well after each addition, then add the cooled melted chocolate and mix gently until just incorporated.

Gently mix in half of the flour mixture, followed by half of the coffee or water. Repeat with the remaining flour mixture and liquid. Spoon the batter into the prepared tin and bake for 50–60 minutes or until a skewer inserted in the centre comes out almost clean – some crumbs are ideal. If there is still wet batter on the skewer, continue cooking until done. Allow to cool completely before removing the cake from the tin.

Dust with extra cocoa powder and serve.

On my last trip to Italy, I was introduced to this wonderful method of cooking chestnuts. Having only previously eaten them roasted or pureed in sweets or soups, it was a revelation. My friends Roberta and Luca had procured the fattest, most humungous Tuscan chestnuts I had ever seen. Roberta dutifully cut each one with a sharp paring knife and placed them in a large pot. To this she added some wild fennel, a large pinch of salt and enough water to let them boil freely. Once tender, we ate them warm with a glass of Tuscan red wine. Here, I've suggested a few other things you can add to flavour the chestnuts; choose one or all – whatever you add, it is truly a beautiful way to eat the season.

SIMPLE CHESTNUTS

SERVES 8

1 kg chestnuts

large handful of wild fennel or fennel fronds

2 fresh bay leaves

1 strip of orange zest

sea salt

Using a small sharp knife, cut a cross on the round side of each chestnut. Place in a large saucepan along with the fennel, bay leaves, orange zest and a large pinch of salt. Cover with plenty of water and bring to the boil over a high heat. Reduce the heat to medium and simmer until the chestnuts are tender – this might take around 45 minutes but timings will vary, so begin checking as early as 25 minutes. Simply pull out a chestnut with tongs and, when cool enough to handle, peel back the tough exterior – the inside should be nice and tender, similar to the texture of cooked potato. Drain and serve.

WINTER

The cold brings warmth with it, too – warmth from the kitchen and from people gathering inside. The food is hearty, generous and distinctly wintry. There are few greater pleasures than the aroma from a braise bubbling away on the stove or the sight of a cake emerging from the oven on a cool weekend morning. Oranges, lemons and mandarins sit on the table still adorned with their leaves. There is beauty in every season and when we are in the biting depths of winter, fortunately it is food that envelopes and carries us towards spring.

When we're unwell or simply craving some warmth on a frosty morning, congee is what I love to cook. Essentially a rice porridge, the base is usually very straightforward – rice cooked in broth or, even more simply, water. When you get to the toppings you can really mix it up, depending on your tastes or what you have at hand. I love loading up my congee with plenty of ginger, coriander and spring onion, and drizzling with a good spoonful of chilli or sesame oil. I sometimes add a soft-boiled egg or some of the chicken left over from making the broth. I often make this with leftover rice from the night before's dinner, in which case you won't need as much liquid and the cooking time is significantly reduced. To save even more time, simply replace the chicken broth with store-bought stock or some you have tucked away in the freezer. Often eaten at breakfast, congee makes a more than acceptable lunch or dinner, too. Nori loves to eat it plain with a raw egg mixed into the hot rice and topped simply with spring onion and a little soy sauce, which is more like the Japanese version (*okayu*) – his comfort food. We also eat a version called *Nanakusa-gayu* on the seventh of January. It should contain seven different herbs and is a great reprieve from Christmas and New Year feasting.

CONGEE

SERVES 4

220 g (1 cup) white
short-grain rice

sea salt

CHICKEN BROTH

1 chicken frame

100 ml saké

2 cm piece of ginger, bruised

3 garlic cloves, bruised

2 spring onions

sea salt

TOPPINGS

julienned ginger

chilli oil (see page 121) or
sesame oil

coriander leaves

finely sliced spring onion

halved soft-boiled eggs or
soy eggs (see page 54)

For the broth, place all of the ingredients in a stockpot and cover with 4 litres of cold water. Bring to the boil over a high heat, then reduce to a simmer, skimming any impurities from the surface. Cook, half covered, for 1½ hours. Strain the broth through a sieve, discard the solids and season to taste.
You can use the broth immediately or transfer it to an airtight container. The broth will keep in the fridge for up to 3 days or in the freezer for up to 3 months.

Return the broth to the pot (you should have about 3 litres) and add the rice. Cook over a low heat for 45 minutes or until the rice is soft and the soup is thick. Be sure to stir occasionally, especially as it thickens, as the rice will easily catch on the bottom and burn. If the congee looks like it is becoming too dry, add some water. It should be thick but still a little soupy, as it will thicken some more upon cooling. Season to taste, then ladle into bowls and cover with the toppings of your choice.

The key to this salad is in the way you cook the broccoli. The pan needs to be very hot and the broccoli cooked until just tender and nicely charred. Next to the creamy mozzarella, it is completely delightful. Serve this salad with some fresh bread to mop up the dressing.

BROCCOLI AND MOZZARELLA SALAD

SERVES 4

2 heads of broccoli (about 500 g in total), cut into large florets

2 tablespoons extra-virgin olive oil, plus extra for drizzling

sea salt and black pepper

250 g buffalo mozzarella, torn

1 long red chilli, finely sliced

finely grated zest and juice of 1 lemon

Place the broccoli in a large bowl. Drizzle over the olive oil, add a large pinch of sea salt and, using your hands, massage the oil and salt into the broccoli to ensure it is well coated.

Heat a large frying pan or chargrill pan over a high heat and, when smoking, add the broccoli. Cook for around 5 minutes, turning occasionally, until the broccoli is just tender and charred. Transfer to a serving plate and allow to cool briefly. You don't want it to be so hot that the cheese melts.

Add the mozzarella to the broccoli, then scatter with the sliced chilli and lemon zest. Drizzle with the lemon juice and a generous amount of olive oil, season with salt and pepper and serve.

Zuppa alla pavese is a humble soup originating in Pavia in the north of Italy. It relies on good-quality ingredients since there are so few to begin with. While you can use store-bought, it really is worth making your own broth for this soup; the richness is unbeatable. Good bread fried in butter, fresh free-range eggs (preferably organic) and freshly grated *real* parmesan (parmigiano reggiano) are what make this soup special.

ZUPPA ALLA PAVESE

SERVES 4

4 eggs

unsalted butter, for frying

4 slices of sourdough bread

grated parmesan, to serve

roughly chopped parsley leaves, to serve

sea salt and black pepper

BEEF AND CHICKEN BROTH

800 g beef bones

800 g bone-in chicken pieces (you can use wings, drumsticks or thighs)

1 onion, halved

1 carrot, cut into thirds

1 celery stalk, halved

2 peppercorns

2 fresh bay leaves

generous pinch of sea salt

For the broth, place all of the ingredients in a stockpot and cover with about 4 litres of cold water. Bring to the boil over a high heat, then reduce to a gentle simmer, skimming any impurities from the surface (this is especially important in the first 15 minutes). Cover with a lid and cook for 3–4 hours. Strain the broth through a sieve and discard the solids or set aside for another use. Season to taste. You can use the broth immediately or transfer it to an airtight container. The broth will keep in the fridge for up to 3 days or in the freezer for up to 3 months.

When ready to eat, have the broth simmering gently on the stove. Poach the eggs either in the broth or in water, following the instructions on page 227. Remove with a slotted spoon and drain on paper towel.

Heat the butter in a large frying pan over a medium heat and, when foaming, fry the sourdough for 2 minutes on each side or until golden.

Divide the fried sourdough among four bowls, top each with a poached egg and ladle over the hot broth. Top with plenty of the grated parmesan and a sprinkling of parsley. Season with salt and pepper and serve immediately.

This salad is one of my midweek staples and is really simple to put together. The herbs are what really bring this dish to life, so be generous. While I wouldn't replace the lentils in this salad, the quinoa can definitely be substituted with another grain, such as barley, brown rice or millet – just be mindful that cooking times will vary. Feel free to use canned lentils if you're short on time.

LENTIL AND MAPLE-ROASTED CARROT SALAD

SERVES 4–6

150 g puy lentils, soaked overnight and drained

100 g quinoa, rinsed

2 celery stalks, finely sliced

large handful each of coriander, mint and parsley leaves

100 g baby spinach leaves, roughly chopped

70 g (½ cup) toasted hazelnuts, roughly chopped

1 tablespoon toasted sesame seeds

MAPLE-ROASTED CARROTS

500 g carrots, trimmed

2 tablespoons maple syrup

2 tablespoons extra-virgin olive oil

juice of ½ lemon

2 garlic cloves, bruised

sea salt

ZINGY DRESSING

100 ml extra-virgin olive oil

juice of 2 limes

1 small garlic clove, grated

2 French shallots or ½ red onion, finely chopped

sea salt

Preheat the oven to 180°C. Line a baking tray with baking paper.

For the maple-roasted carrots, first cut the carrots in half crossways and then lengthways. Place in a bowl and pour over the maple syrup, olive oil and lemon juice. Mix with your hands to ensure they are well coated. Add the garlic and season with salt. Tip it all onto the prepared baking tray and roast for 45 minutes or until the carrots are tender and golden. Set aside to cool.

Meanwhile, cook the lentils and quinoa in separate saucepans of boiling water until tender, approximately 25 and 15 minutes, respectively. Drain and set aside to cool.

For the dressing, whisk the olive oil, lime juice, garlic and shallot or onion together in a small bowl and season to taste with salt.

In a large bowl, combine the cooled lentils and quinoa, roasted carrots, celery, herbs, spinach leaves, hazelnuts and sesame seeds. Pour the dressing over the salad, toss to combine and serve.

There is something so soothing about making bread. In exchange for just a little bit of effort and some time, very basic ingredients turn into something rather special. Focaccia is an especially simple bread to make, too – it's freeform and very forgiving. This particular version is inspired by the focaccia you find in Italy's southern region of Puglia and, more specifically, its capital, Bari. Mashed potato is added to the dough to create the most soft and pillowy bread. In this recipe, I've suggested a topping of taleggio and potato (pictured overleaf), but you can leave the focaccia plain with just olive oil and salt, or top with things like olives, onion, herbs or cherry tomatoes.

FOCACCIA

SERVES 6–8

1 waxy potato (150 g), peeled and roughly chopped

200 g semolina flour (see page 12)

300 g tipo 00 flour

5 g active dry yeast

10 g fine sea salt

350 ml warm water

extra-virgin olive oil, for drizzling

POTATO AND TALEGGIO TOPPING (OPTIONAL)

150 g taleggio, roughly sliced or torn into pieces

2 waxy potatoes, finely sliced on a mandoline

sea salt

rosemary, to garnish

Cook the potato in a small saucepan of boiling water until very tender. Drain and allow to cool briefly, then mash until smooth and set aside.

Meanwhile, combine the flours, yeast and salt in the bowl of a stand mixer fitted with a dough hook. Mix together on medium speed, add the potato and then the warm water in a steady stream. Increase the speed to high and mix for 10 minutes until the dough is smooth, elastic and soft, but not sticky. (Alternatively, mix everything together by hand, then turn out onto a floured board and knead until smooth.) Place the dough in an oiled bowl and either cover and leave in a warm place for 1 hour until the dough has doubled in size, or place in the fridge to rise overnight (I highly recommend this method if you have time, as it allows the flavours to develop and will result in a fluffier, more aerated focaccia). If the dough has risen in the fridge overnight, allow it to come back to room temperature before moving on to the next step.

Preheat the oven to 220°C. Grease a 30 cm round baking tray with olive oil and line with baking paper. (Lining the tray with baking paper is optional, so feel free to just grease the tray directly with olive oil if you prefer; this will result in a slightly crunchier base.

Using your hands or a pastry scraper, tip the dough from the bowl onto the prepared tray. Using your hands, gently spread the dough outwards towards the edge of the tray. Set aside to rise in a warm place for a further 30–45 minutes. The dough should be nice and puffy. If using the topping, gently press pieces of taleggio onto the dough, then cover with the finely sliced potato (alternatively, see the introduction above for other topping suggestions, or just leave plain). Drizzle the focaccia with olive oil and sprinkle with sea salt. Bake for 30 minutes or until golden and cooked through. Scatter the hot focaccia with the rosemary. Allow to cool briefly, then transfer to a wire rack to cool. Focaccia is best eaten on the day it's made.

Winter is perfect soup weather. I love the action of chopping all of the ingredients and setting the pot on the stove to bubble away. This soup fills the house with aromas that, to me, simply smell of home cooking. Leave out the pancetta if you're vegetarian, vegan or just prefer it without; the porcini will give you a lovely depth of flavour anyway. This soup is great to make in advance – I just add the spinach as I'm reheating the soup so that it stays nice and green.

WINTER BARLEY SOUP

SERVES 4

3 tablespoons extra-virgin olive oil, plus extra to serve

1 onion, finely chopped

1 celery stalk, finely chopped

1 carrot, finely chopped

sea salt

1 potato, roughly chopped

4 garlic cloves, roughly chopped

4 sage leaves

60 g pancetta, halved

120 g pearl barley

10 g dried porcini, soaked in 100 ml warm water for 15 minutes

1.5 litres vegetable or chicken stock

2 fresh bay leaves

150 g English or baby spinach leaves, tough stems removed and leaves roughly torn

crusty bread, to serve

Warm the olive oil in a large saucepan over a low heat. Gently fry the onion, celery and carrot with a pinch of salt for about 10–15 minutes until soft and beginning to colour. Add the potato, garlic and sage leaves and cook for a few more minutes until the garlic is fragrant and everything has mingled together nicely. Now add the pancetta, barley and the porcini and soaking liquid. Pour in the stock and pop in the bay leaves. Allow to simmer for 30–35 minutes until the soup has thickened and the pearl barley is very tender. Remove the pancetta and cut into lardons. Return to the pan along with the spinach and continue to simmer for about 2 minutes until the spinach has wilted. Season to taste.

Ladle the soup into bowls and serve with an extra drizzle of olive oil and some crusty bread.

Although I once had a strong dislike for anchovies, now I can and do eat them straight from their small and beautifully decorated tins. Be sure to buy the best anchovies you can find – it's completely worth it.

The pissaladière is a masterful balance of flavours and textures: the natural sweetness of the onions (which do take a while to cook, I know), the saltiness of the anchovies and olives, and the buttery flaky pastry work in complete harmony. Pissaladière is sometimes made on a pizza-type base, but I prefer this version. If you're short on time, store-bought puff pastry works well, too.

PISSALADIÈRE

SERVES 4–6

125 ml (½ cup) extra-virgin olive oil

3 onions, finely sliced

sea salt

12 anchovy fillets

80 g pitted black olives

1 egg, lightly beaten

FLAKY PASTRY

250 g (1⅔ cups) plain flour

fine sea salt

125 g chilled unsalted butter, cut into cubes

3 tablespoons iced water

To make the pastry dough, tip the flour onto a clean work surface and sprinkle over a pinch of salt. Add the butter and toss so that all the pieces are coated. Rub the butter into the flour using your fingertips until the mixture has the consistency of very coarse breadcrumbs (it should look rather pebbly). Sprinkle over the water and bring the flour and butter together with your hands until there are no dry crumbs left. Flatten into a rough circle and cover with plastic wrap. Refrigerate for around 30 minutes.

Preheat the oven to 180°C. Line a 25 cm round baking tray with baking paper.

Warm the olive oil in a large frying pan over a low–medium heat. Add the onion with a small pinch of salt and cook, stirring occasionally, for around 30 minutes until the onion is soft and gently caramelised. Season to taste and set aside to cool. Don't over-salt the onion – you want it to remain sweet as a contrast to the olives and anchovies.

On a lightly floured work surface, roll out the pastry to a 28 cm round, about 2 mm thick. Drape the pastry over the prepared tray, spread with the cooled onion mixture, then top with the anchovies and olives. Fold in the overhanging pastry edge to create a border, crimping as you go. Whisk 1 teaspoon of water into the egg. Brush the edge of the pissaladière with the egg wash, then bake for 40 minutes or until the pastry is golden. Allow to cool slightly before serving, however, it is equally delicious served at room temperature.

My mum would make baked pasta for us a lot when we were kids – I can remember it so clearly. She would cut into it at the table and serve large squares onto our plates. I think she made it because it was, of course, delicious, but also incredibly simple, affordable and comforting, too. I usually prefer oven-cooked food during the week, because it can be happily cooking away while I attend to other things. This version is a little different to the traditional Maltese one I grew up eating – it's considerably lighter and meat-free (although the addition of a few pork and fennel sausages squeezed from their casing, rolled into small meatballs and fried off with the garlic is delicious, too). It's a perfect meal for when the fridge is looking a little bare.

WEEKNIGHT BAKED MACCHERONI

SERVES 6

3 tablespoons extra-virgin olive oil

1 onion, finely chopped

sea salt

3 garlic cloves, roughly chopped

1.2 kg canned whole peeled tomatoes

small handful of basil leaves

500 g dried short pasta, such as rigatoni, macaroni or penne

300 g buffalo mozzarella or fior di latte, roughly torn

200 g mozzarella, grated

50 g parmesan or pecorino, grated

Preheat the oven to 180°C. Grease a 23 cm baking dish with butter.

Warm the olive oil in a large frying pan over a low–medium heat. Add the onion and a pinch of salt and gently cook for around 10 minutes until soft and sweet. Add the garlic and cook for a further 2 minutes. Add the tomatoes and basil and simmer for 15 minutes, breaking up the tomatoes with the back of a wooden spoon. Season to taste.

Meanwhile, cook the pasta in a large saucepan of generously salted boiling water for half the cooking time instructed on the packet. Drain and stir the pasta through the sauce along with both types of mozzarella.

Tumble the pasta mixture into the prepared baking dish. Scatter over the parmesan and bake for 15–20 minutes or until the pasta is tender and the edges are bubbling. If the top is browning too fast, cover with foil.

This is delicious served hot, but equally as lovely warm.

The secret to this ragù is the smallest amount of milk, which gives the sauce a lovely richness and, at the same time, mellows the fattiness of the lamb. I particularly love serving this ragù with large, ostentatious rigatoni – the ridges are very good at catching the sauce – but other shapes like penne and fusilli would be fine, too. Try and find authentic pecorino made with sheep's milk. It has the perfect sharpness and saltiness.

RIGATONI WITH LAMB RAGÙ

SERVES 4

3 tablespoons extra-virgin olive oil

1 onion, finely diced

1 celery stalk, finely diced

2 garlic cloves, finely chopped

½ teaspoon finely chopped rosemary leaves

1 teaspoon ground allspice

sea salt

400 g lamb mince

200 g canned whole peeled tomatoes

100 ml chicken or vegetable stock

2½ tablespoons full-cream milk

320 g dried rigatoni or other short pasta

grated pecorino, to serve

Warm the olive oil in a large frying pan over a low–medium heat. Gently fry the onion, celery and garlic for around 15 minutes, stirring occasionally, until soft and beginning to colour. Add the rosemary, allspice and a generous pinch of salt and cook for a further 2 minutes until fragrant. Increase the heat to high and add the mince, breaking it up with the back of a wooden spoon. Cook for around 10 minutes until the mince has browned off nicely, then add the canned tomatoes and stock. Simmer for 25–30 minutes, then stir in the milk and cook for a further 5 minutes. Keep warm over a very low heat.

Cook the rigatoni in a large saucepan of generously salted water for a minute or two less than the cooking time instructed on the packet until just under al dente. Drain the pasta, reserving 250 ml (1 cup) of the cooking water. Increase the heat under the sauce to medium and, when bubbling again, add the pasta along with some of the reserved cooking water. Cook the pasta in the sauce for 1–2 minutes until al dente. If the sauce is too dry, add more pasta cooking water as needed.

Serve with a generous scattering of grated pecorino.

Sausages are the key to this quick, flavourful pasta sauce. Because the sausages themselves are already seasoned, very little needs to be done to make the sauce delicious. Cavatelli is a small hollowed pasta made from semolina flour and water that comes in many different incarnations. They can be made short, using one finger to roll, or longer, which uses three or four fingers. Making them is rather simple, albeit a little time-consuming, but they are also readily available from Italian grocers or specialty supermarkets. Use 320 grams of store-bought cavatelli, or another shape such as casarecce or orecchiette, and cook for a minute or two less than the packet instructions say to.

CAVATELLI WITH SAUSAGE AND CAVOLO NERO

SERVES 4

3 tablespoons extra-virgin olive oil

1 onion, finely diced

3 garlic cloves, finely chopped

6 sage leaves

pinch of dried chilli flakes, plus extra to serve

3 pork and fennel sausages (about 300 g), casings removed

400 g canned whole peeled tomatoes

1 bunch of cavolo nero (about 150 g), tough stems removed, leaves washed thoroughly and roughly chopped

sea salt

grated parmesan, to serve

CAVATELLI

400 g semolina flour (see page 12), plus extra for dusting

fine sea salt

180 ml warm water

To make the dough for the cavatelli, tip the flour onto a clean work surface and mix with a large pinch of salt. Make a well in the centre and slowly pour in the warm water. If the dough feels very dry or difficult to bring together, sprinkle over a little extra water. Using your hands, bring a little flour at a time into the water until you have a rough dough. Use a pastry scraper to bring it all together and pick up any bits of dough on the board. Knead for about 10 minutes until smooth. Cover with plastic wrap or an upturned bowl and set aside for at least 30 minutes.

Divide the pasta dough into four pieces. Take one piece, keeping the remainder covered while you work, and, on a lightly floured work surface, roll it into a rope about 1.5 cm thick. Cut the rope into 1 cm lengths and use a finger to press down and roll the piece of dough to create a small cavern. This is best done on a flat wooden board, or use a ridged gnocchi board for more texture. Place the shaped cavatelli onto a board or tea towel generously dusted with semolina flour. Repeat the process with the rest of the pasta dough, arranging the cavatelli in a single layer to ensure they don't stick to each other.

Warm the olive oil in a large frying pan over a low–medium heat. Add the onion and fry gently for about 15 minutes until soft and beginning to colour. Stir in the garlic, sage and dried chilli. Increase the heat to medium–high and add the sausage meat. Break up the meat with the back of a wooden spoon and cook for 3–4 minutes until nicely golden. Add the tomatoes and simmer for 5 minutes, then stir through the cavolo nero and cook for a further 15 minutes. Season to taste and keep warm.

Meanwhile, cook the pasta in a large saucepan of generously salted water for 3–4 minutes, or until just under al dente. Drain the pasta, reserving 250 ml (1 cup) of the cooking water. Increase the heat under the sauce to medium and, when bubbling again, add the pasta along with some of the reserved cooking water and cook for 1–2 minutes until the pasta is al dente and well coated. If the sauce is too dry, add more cooking water as needed. Serve with plenty of grated parmesan and extra chilli flakes.

These little pork and cabbage dumplings are a family favourite. I love cooking a meal that gets everyone involved – we all sit around the table, folding and rolling. It's a great way to pass the time when the weather is less than desirable, too. We make our own gyoza wrappers at home, so we decide exactly what goes into the dough, but, of course, store-bought ones are the next best thing – you will need about 35 for this amount of filling. The crimping takes a little practice, but once you get the hang of it, it really is very simple – and there is no need for them to be perfect. Similarly with the frying, at first it may seem counterintuitive to fry the gyoza in oil, then to add water, but this ensures each dumpling has a crispy bottom while the water steams and subsequently cooks the dumplings. We eat these for dinner simply with steamed rice.

PORK AND CABBAGE GYOZA

SERVES 4–6

½ wombok (about 300 g), finely sliced

2 teaspoons sea salt

4 spring onions, finely sliced, plus extra to serve

3 garlic cloves, finely grated

3 cm piece of ginger, finely grated

handful of coriander leaves, finely chopped

500 g pork mince

1 tablespoon caster sugar

3 tablespoons soy sauce

2 tablespoons sesame oil

vegetable oil, for frying

sea salt and white pepper

shichimi togarashi, to serve

GYOZA WRAPPERS

250 g (1⅔ cups) plain flour, plus extra for dusting

125–150 ml boiling water

CONTINUED OVERLEAF →

To make the dough for the gyoza wrappers, place the flour in a large bowl of a stand mixer fitted with a dough hook. Slowly pour in the boiling water (start with 125 ml and add more if needed) and mix on a medium speed for 10 minutes, or until the dough is soft and elastic. It shouldn't come together in a ball, it is too soft for that, but it also shouldn't be pasty. Add 1 tablespoon of extra flour if the mixture seems wet. Dust the dough in flour, then wrap in plastic wrap and allow to rest for 30 minutes.

Meanwhile, toss the cabbage in a bowl with the salt and set aside to drain for 15 minutes. Squeeze the salted cabbage to remove any excess liquid. Combine the spring onion, garlic, ginger, coriander, pork, sugar, soy sauce and sesame oil in the bowl of a stand mixer fitted with a paddle attachment. Beat on a low speed for 2–3 minutes until the mixture is well incorporated and almost paste-like in texture. Add the cabbage and mix again for 30 seconds just to incorporate. Alternatively, mix well using a wooden spoon or your hands.

To make the gyoza wrappers, roll the dough into a 1.5 cm thick log and then cut into 1 cm lengths. You will need to generously flour your work surface when doing this. It's handy to keep a small mound of flour on the bench that you can then just drag into the centre as you need. There is no need to roll and cut all of the dough, either – just cut off as much as you can work with in a short time, keeping the remainder of the dough covered so it doesn't dry out. Working with one piece at a time, face the dough cut-side up and roll into a 7–8 cm round using a rolling pin. The easiest way to create a circle shape is to turn the piece 90 degrees each time you do a roll. Lightly dust the wrappers with flour and set aside as you continue with the remainder of the dough. If the wrappers will be sitting out for some time, cover them with a tea towel or plastic wrap.

CONTINUED OVERLEAF →

SOY AND VINEGAR DIPPING SAUCE

3 tablespoons soy sauce

3 tablespoons rice vinegar

pinch of shichimi togarashi or dried chilli flakes, or serve with a dash of chilli oil (see page 121)

Line a baking tray with baking paper and fill a small bowl with water. Now you're ready to assemble.

Hold a gyoza wrapper in one hand and place about a tablespoon of the pork mixture in the centre. Dip a finger in the bowl of water and use it to dampen all around the edge of the gyoza wrapper. Fold the wrapper to lightly envelope the mixture, as if you were holding a taco. Using both hands, pinch the gyoza edges together and make a small crimp. Make small pleats, from the middle out, until completely sealed. Place the dumpling on the lined tray and repeat with remaining gyoza wrappers and pork mixture.

For the dipping sauce, combine the ingredients in a small bowl and set aside.

Heat 1 tablespoon of vegetable oil in large heavy-based frying pan over a medium–high heat and add the gyoza in a single layer, fairly tightly packed and flat-side down. You will need to do this in batches or multiple frying pans. Cook for about 3 minutes until the bottoms of the gyoza are crispy and golden. Add 200 ml of water to the pan and cover with a lid (be careful when adding the water as it will bubble and spit as soon as it hits the hot oil). Steam the gyoza for about 7 minutes, or until the liquid has completely evaporated and the dumplings are cooked through.

Season the gyoza with salt and white pepper and serve with a scattering of extra spring onion and shichimi togarashi and the dipping sauce alongside.

Panissa alla vercellese or panissa rice is like a heartier cousin of risotto. It has rice, as the name suggests, but also beans and sausage (traditionally, it uses a fresh salami which is near impossible to source outside of Italy, so regular pork sausages are a fine substitute). Panissa rice hails from the province of Vercelli, a region surrounded by rice fields. If you can find it, seek out Carnaroli rice, which is particular to the area and well suited to this dish, and risotto in general, as it keeps its shape nicely once cooked. This is a complete meal and so comforting in the depths of winter.

PANISSA RICE

SERVES 4–6

1.5 litres chicken or vegetable stock, or other meat broth

150 g dried borlotti beans, soaked overnight and drained

2 tablespoons extra-virgin olive oil, plus extra to serve

1 onion, finely sliced

4 pork sausages (about 400 g), casings removed

250 g Carnaroli or other risotto rice

1 tablespoon tomato paste

200 ml dry red wine

60 g grated parmesan, plus extra to serve

sea salt

marjoram leaves, to serve

Bring the stock to the boil in a saucepan over a high heat and add the drained beans. Reduce to a simmer and cook for about 30 minutes, or until the beans are tender but still a little firm. Remove the beans from the stock using a slotted spoon and set aside. Keep the stock warm over a low heat.

Meanwhile, heat the olive oil in a large heavy-based saucepan over a medium heat and fry the onion for about 8 minutes until soft and light amber in colour. Break the sausages into large pieces and fry until golden on all sides. Try not to disturb them too much as you want them to stay in pieces, rather than breaking up into mince. Add the rice and stir constantly for 3 minutes, or until the rice is opaque and well coated. Add the tomato paste and stir to coat the rice. Pour in the wine and simmer until the rice has absorbed all of the liquid. Add the cooked beans and half of the stock. Simmer over a low–medium heat, stirring occasionally. Once the liquid has been absorbed, add the remaining stock and continue to cook, stirring, for 15–20 minutes until the rice is al dente. The rice should still be quite wet, but less so than a risotto, which is more fluid.

Stir in the parmesan, season to taste and serve with topped with more grated parmesan, an extra drizzle of olive oil and a scattering of marjoram.

Lasagne is a subjective thing. Every family has their own interpretation. This recipe is for my mother, who used to make innumerable trays of lasagne for our family when we were young. Her version was rather different, though – she would beat eggs with cream and pour it into the lasagne. The layers would set almost firm once out of the oven. Sometimes she would add ricotta and never, ever did I see her make a béchamel. Mine, well, here it is: a simple ragù, which I usually make the day before to develop the flavour (but also for convenience); fresh pasta, blanched for just a minute; the most simple béchamel; and plenty of parmesan and mozzarella. You can make it exactly like this, or tweak and adapt to suit your own table. Store-bought dried lasagne sheets are fine, but you will need to make sure your ragù is a little runnier than my recipe calls for as the dried sheets tend to be thirstier than their fresh counterparts. This recipe can most certainly be doubled and made into two lasagnes (perfect for freezing) or one larger tray for feeding a crowd. Lasagne is very simple, you just need to allow enough time to make the different elements. A perfect weekend project when the weather is more suited to pottering around the house.

LASAGNE

SERVES 6

100 g parmesan, grated

300 g buffalo mozzarella or fior di latte, roughly torn

250 g scamorza or mozzarella (or a combination of both), grated

50 g unsalted butter, roughly chopped

sage leaves, to garnish

RAGÙ

3 tablespoons extra-virgin olive oil

1 onion, finely chopped

1 celery stalk, finely chopped

1 kg mince (equal parts beef, pork and veal)

sea salt and black pepper

250 ml (1 cup) dry white wine

2 sage sprigs

3 oregano sprigs

2 basil sprigs

700 g tomato passata

50 g unsalted butter

CONTINUED OVERLEAF →

For the ragù, warm the olive oil in a large frying pan over a low–medium heat. Fry the onion and celery for about 10 minutes until soft and beginning to colour. Increase the heat to high and add the mince. Season with salt and pepper and cook until the mince is nicely browned, breaking up any lumps with the back of a wooden spoon. Pour in the wine, then add the herbs, passata and butter along with 300 ml of water. Bring to a simmer, then reduce the heat to low and cook gently for 1½ hours. Remove and discard any stems from the herb sprigs and season to taste. If making a day in advance, allow to cool before transferring to an airtight container and storing in the fridge.

For the pasta dough, tip the flour onto a clean work surface and scatter over the salt. Make a well in the centre and crack in the eggs. Gently whisk the eggs using a fork, then slowly bring in the flour and incorporate, mixing in a circular motion. When the mixture becomes too thick to mix with the fork, use your hands, with the help of a pastry scraper, to bring it all together. Knead for about 10 minutes until the dough is smooth and elastic. Flatten into a disc, cover with plastic wrap or an upturned bowl and set aside for at least 30 minutes.

Preheat the oven to 180°C. Lightly grease the base of a 25 cm x 30 cm baking dish with butter.

Divide the pasta dough into four pieces. Cover three of the pieces and set aside. On a lightly floured work surface, roll out the dough using a rolling pin into a rough disc around 5 mm thick. Roll the dough through a pasta machine set to the widest setting, then roll again through the next two narrower settings, dusting with a little flour between each roll if needed. Fold the dough back in on itself so it's a bit narrower than the width of the machine and use a rolling pin to flatten slightly. Set the machine back to the widest setting and roll back through the first settings again, folding and flattening the pasta dough before each roll.

CONTINUED OVERLEAF →

LASAGNE SHEETS

400 g tipo 00 flour,
plus extra for dusting

pinch of fine sea salt

4 eggs

BÉCHAMEL

75 g unsalted butter

75 g (½ cup) plain flour

750 ml (3 cups) full-cream milk

generous pinch of freshly
grated nutmeg

sea salt

Repeat this process two more times, so you've rolled the dough through the widest settings, folding between each roll, three times in total. This makes the pasta nice and strong, and you can now roll the dough through the settings until the pasta is around 1.5 mm thick. Repeat with the remaining pieces of dough. Cut into lengths to fit your baking dish then blanch the pasta in salted boiling water for 1 minute. Arrange the sheets on clean tea towels with enough space to prevent them from sticking.

For the béchamel, melt the butter in a large heavy-based saucepan over a medium heat. When the butter is foaming, add the flour and stir constantly with a wooden spoon for 2 minutes to cook the flour. Now swap to a whisk and slowly pour in the milk, whisking as you go to avoid any lumps. Continue whisking until the sauce becomes thick like pouring custard. Add the nutmeg and season lightly with salt.

If you've made the ragù in advance, reheat in a saucepan over a medium heat to make it easier to layer.

To assemble, cover the base of the baking dish with a large spoonful each of the ragù and béchamel. Now add a layer of pasta, followed by layers of the ragù, béchamel and cheeses. Repeat four more times, finishing with a layer of béchamel, cheese, a few dots of butter and some sage leaves. The lasagne can be baked immediately, or you can cover, refrigerate and bake within 24 hours.

Bake for 25–30 minutes, or until the edges are bubbling and the top is golden. If the lasagne is cold from the fridge, increase the cooking time to 35–40 minutes. Allow to rest for at least 30 minutes before serving.

This is such a family favourite of ours and something I've been eating since I was little. My mum would make the Maltese version, bragioli, and serve it with mashed potatoes and peas. There are plenty of variations of these little beef rolls. The fillings change depending on what is available and they are often made with veal or even chicken. I've chosen topside beef for mine, but ask your butcher which cut they recommend on the day. You want something that is large enough to be rolled up to encase the filling. Here, I've suggested serving it with crusty bread, but it is also incredible on soft polenta or mashed potatoes, as my mum would serve it with.

BEEF INVOLTINI

SERVES 4–6

60 g (½ cup) raisins, chopped

70 g pine nuts

80 g (1 cup) fresh breadcrumbs (see Note page 33)

handful of parsley leaves, finely chopped

6 sage leaves, finely chopped, plus extra leaves to serve

1 garlic clove, finely grated

50 g pecorino, finely grated

sea salt and black pepper

8–12 pieces (800 g) of thinly sliced topside beef, gently pounded flat

8–12 thin slices of prosciutto

2 tablespoons extra-virgin olive oil

crusty bread, to serve

SAUCE

3 tablespoons extra-virgin olive oil

1 onion, finely diced

1 celery stalk, finely diced

1 small carrot, finely diced

700 g tomato passata

1 fresh bay leaf

sea salt

For the sauce, warm the olive oil in a large deep frying pan or flameproof casserole dish over medium heat. Gently fry the onion, celery and carrot for around 15 minutes until soft and beginning to caramelise ever so slightly. Add the passata, bay leaf and 200 ml of water and simmer for 10 minutes until slightly thickened. Season with salt and keep warm.

Meanwhile, prepare the involtini by first making the filling. In a large bowl, combine the raisins, pine nuts, breadcrumbs, parsley, sage, garlic and pecorino. Season with salt and a little pepper.

Lay the pieces of beef out flat and cover each one with a slice of prosciutto. Scatter some filling over each piece of prosciutto, distributing it evenly among all the slices, and roll up from the shortest side. Fasten each involtini with a skewer or toothpick.

Heat another frying pan over a medium–high heat, then add the olive oil and sear the involtini on all sides. They don't need to be deeply coloured, but a little golden is ideal.

Return the pan with the sauce to a medium heat and nestle the involtini into the sauce, spooning some of it over the involtini to cover. Simmer, covered, for 25–30 minutes, turning the involtini halfway. The beef should still be tender and the sauce nicely thickened. Season the sauce with extra salt and pepper, if necessary, and serve with a scattering of extra sage leaves and some crusty bread.

I love the simplicity of this pasta. It's fresh and zingy and has wonderful texture thanks to the almonds and breadcrumbs. You could top the pasta with a scattering of parmesan, but with the breadcrumbs, you really don't need to. Omit the anchovies to make it vegetarian.

CAULIFLOWER PASTA

SERVES 4

300 g cauliflower, cut into small florets

3 tablespoons extra-virgin olive oil

6 garlic cloves, finely chopped

½ long red chilli, deseeded and finely chopped

3 anchovy fillets

320 g dried short pasta, such as paccheri, calamarata or penne

50 g (⅓ cup) toasted almonds, roughly chopped

finely grated zest of 1 lemon

CRUNCHY BREADCRUMBS

2 tablespoons extra-virgin olive oil

100 g (1¼ cups) fresh breadcrumbs (see Note page 33)

sea salt

Bring a large saucepan of salted water to the boil and cook the cauliflower for 10–15 minutes until tender. Remove with a slotted spoon and set aside. Don't drain the water, as you'll cook the pasta in the same pan.

Meanwhile, for the crunchy breadcrumbs, heat the olive oil in a frying pan over a medium heat. Add the breadcrumbs and stir to coat, then continue to stir and cook for about 5 minutes until they are golden and crunchy. Remove from the heat, season with salt and set aside to cool.

Warm the olive oil in a large frying pan over a low heat and gently cook the garlic, chilli and anchovies for 3–4 minutes, stirring often to stop them burning. Add the cauliflower and a ladleful of the cooking water and simmer for about 5 minutes until the cauliflower is very tender.

Meanwhile, bring the cauliflower cooking water back to the boil and cook the pasta for a minute or two less than the packet instructions until just under al dente. Using a slotted spoon, transfer the pasta to the cauliflower mixture and stir to combine. If the sauce is dry, add another ladleful of cooking water. Increase the heat to high and cook, stirring the pasta, for 1–2 minutes until everything is well coated and the pasta is al dente. Stir through the almonds and lemon zest and serve topped with plenty of crunchy breadcrumbs.

Buta no kakuni, or braised pork, is, I think, one of the most comforting winter dishes. It was a complete revelation when my husband, Nori, cooked this for me for the first time – the flavours and textures were something I had never experienced before. I watched in awe as he trimmed the sharp edges of the daikon to make them slightly rounded – so it would cook evenly. Feel free to do this, but it is by no means a make or break step. There are a few other tricks to make a great buta no kakuni – blanching the pork to remove impurities, and making a caramel to coat the pork, but overall, this dish is very quick to prepare. The pork and daikon gently simmer, absorbing all of the wonderful flavours, and later, soft-boiled eggs are added. It is best left to sit in the fridge for several hours after making. The excess fat will solidify and can then be scraped off for a lighter, more pure braise before being reheated. We eat this simply with wilted greens and steamed rice.

JAPANESE BRAISED PORK

SERVES 4

800 g pork belly, cut into
3 cm cubes

2 tablespoons extra-virgin
olive oil

3 tablespoons caster sugar

3 garlic cloves, chopped

3 cm piece of ginger,
finely sliced

3 spring onions, green
parts only

125 ml (½ cup) saké

80 ml (⅓ cup) soy sauce

1 star anise

1 daikon, peeled, halved
lengthways, then cut into
2 cm thick slices

4 soft-boiled eggs, peeled

Place the pork in a large saucapan and cover with cold water. Bring to the boil over a high heat. As soon as the water begins to boil, drain and set the pork aside.

Heat a large heavy-based frying pan or cast-iron pot over a high heat and pour in the olive oil. Add the pork belly and fry for 1–2 minutes on each side until golden. Remove the pork, then add the sugar and 3 tablespoons of water (be careful as it will spit a little). Simmer for 5–7 minutes, stirring to dissolve the sugar, until you have a deep amber–coloured caramel. Return the pork to the pan and stir to coat, then add the garlic, ginger, spring onion, saké, soy sauce, star anise, daikon and 750 ml (3 cups) of water. Bring to a simmer, then reduce the heat to low and cook for 1–1½ hours until the pork is tender. Nestle the eggs in the pan among the pork and daikon and continue to cook for another 10 minutes.

Secondary cuts of meat, such as ribs, are not only more affordable but they have so much flavour. Yes, they do usually take longer to cook and often require a little more care than a prime cut, but it is so worth it. That said, these braised short ribs require very little active cooking time, you just leave them to simmer away on the stove. Because the ribs are rather rich, I like to pair them with a simple cucumber salad as a way to freshen up the meal. If you're making this dish in the depths of winter, and cucumbers aren't around, you could substitute some sliced wombok. The beef is also delicious stuffed into bao buns, which I keep in the freezer for steaming at short notice.

BRAISED SHORT RIBS

SERVES 4

2 tablespoons extra-virgin olive oil

1.2 kg beef short ribs

sea salt

1 French shallot, chopped

4 garlic cloves, bruised

3 cm piece of ginger, sliced

250 ml (1 cup) saké

500 ml (2 cups) beef or chicken stock

100 ml soy sauce

100 ml mirin

100 ml rice wine vinegar

2 tablespoons brown sugar

1 star anise

steamed rice, to serve

QUICK CUCUMBER SALAD

1 Lebanese cucumber, roughly chopped

2 spring onions, sliced on the diagonal

1 tablespoon toasted sesame seeds

2 tablespoons sesame oil

1 tablespoon rice wine vinegar

sea salt

Heat the olive oil in a large heavy-based saucepan or cast-iron pot with a lid over a high heat. Season the ribs with a generous pinch of salt, then sear on all sides until golden. Remove the ribs and drain all but 1 tablespoon of oil from the pan.

Fry the shallot, garlic and ginger for 3 minutes until coloured, then pour in the saké and allow to simmer for 2 minutes. Return the ribs to the pan, along with the remaining ingredients (except for the rice), then bring to a simmer and cook, covered, over a low heat for 3 hours or until the meat is falling off the bone.

Meanwhile, for the salad, combine the cucumber, spring onion and sesame seeds in a small bowl. Whisk together the sesame oil, vinegar and a large pinch of salt in another small bowl and pour over the salad. Stir to coat and leave to sit for a few minutes before serving.

Remove the beef ribs from the pan and transfer to a serving bowl. Strain the sauce into a small saucepan, returning the aromatics to the beef, and simmer the sauce over a medium heat for 3–4 minutes to thicken slightly. Pour the sauce over the beef and serve with steamed rice and the cucumber salad.

Porchetta, for us, is definitely a celebratory meal. I'll often prepare it for birthdays (many of which, in our family, fall in winter) or for Christmas lunch. In Italy, particularly in Rome – and especially in Ariccia – porchetta is a street food. Delis and small kiosk-type shops sell porchetta that have been cooked for around eight hours in a wood-fired oven or over coals. Sliced and stuffed into a panino or in between some pizza bianca, it is juicy and incredibly flavourful. Traditionally, porchetta is a whole pig deboned and stuffed, which is rather difficult to do at home. Here, I've opted for a large piece of pork belly instead. While you can't get the exact flavour of the porchetta you find in Rome – something about it being in Rome, perhaps – making it at home is very rewarding. If you're not confident tying up the pork yourself, make friends with your local butcher and take your seasoning in so they can tie it up for you. The low temperature followed by the burst of heat at the end will give you crispy, almost glass-like crackling, which should be chopped up with the meat. Serve with roast potatoes or stuffed into panini along with the salsa verde.

PORCHETTA

SERVES 12–15

1 x 2.8–3 kg piece of pork belly (rump end) or deboned shoulder, skin scored

SEASONING

2 tablespoons sea salt

1½ tablespoons fennel seeds, freshly ground

2 tablespoons finely chopped sage leaves

2 tablespoons finely chopped rosemary leaves

4 garlic cloves, finely chopped

1 teaspoon freshly ground black pepper

1 teaspoon dried chilli flakes

SALSA VERDE

1 garlic clove

small bunch of parsley, leaves picked

1 tablespoon salted capers, rinsed

2 anchovy fillets

juice of 1 lemon

approximately 125 ml (½ cup) extra-virgin olive oil

sea salt

Ensure the pork is nice and dry by patting down the skin and flesh with paper towel. Lay the pork, skin-side down, on a clean work surface. Mix all of the seasoning ingredients together in a bowl and rub into the flesh. Roll up the belly and tie tightly using butcher's twine. This can be done the night before and left to rest in the fridge – in fact, I prefer to do this ahead of time to let the flavours get acquainted. I then allow the pork to come to room temperature before moving onto the cooking.

Preheat the oven to 170°C.

Place the pork on a wire rack over a baking tray and roast for 3 hours. Increase the temperature to 200°C, then cook for a further 30 minutes, or until the skin is crackling and golden. Remove and allow to rest for 30 minutes.

Meanwhile, for the salsa verde, finely chop the garlic, then add the parsley and continue to chop, adding the capers and anchovies and continuing to chop until everything is roughly incorporated. Transfer to a small bowl, squeeze in the lemon juice and mix in enough olive oil so that sauce is a drizzling consistency. Season to taste.

Cut the porchetta into slices and serve with the salsa verde.

The beginning of winter still feels rather autumnal, and apples and walnuts continue to feature heavily at the markets – although they will soon give way to citrus and kiwi and other more wintry fruits. Even though this cake has equal proportions of almonds and walnuts, the latter is more pronounced in flavour, and so it is an apple and walnut cake. Buy locally grown walnuts, if possible, or at least local-ish. Imported walnuts are usually very old and are often extremely bitter and not pleasant at all. I usually bake with granny smiths, but if there is another apple variety you prefer, go for it.

APPLE AND WALNUT CAKE

SERVES 8–10

250 g unsalted butter, softened

250 g caster sugar

3 eggs

1 vanilla pod, split and seeds scraped, or 1 teaspoon vanilla bean paste

finely grated zest of 1 lemon

200 g (1⅓ cups) self-raising flour, sifted

100 g (⅔ cup) almonds, finely ground (see Note)

100 g (1 cup) walnuts, finely ground

100 ml full-cream milk

3 granny smith apples (about 400 g in total), peeled, cored and cut into 3 mm thick slices

icing sugar, for dusting (optional)

Preheat the oven to 180°C. Grease a 21 cm round cake tin with butter and line with baking paper.

Cream the butter and sugar together, either using a wooden spoon or a stand mixer fitted with a paddle attachment, until pale and fluffy. Add the eggs, one at a time, beating well between each addition. Add the vanilla and lemon zest and mix to combine. Working in small batches, alternately add the flour, ground nuts and milk, mixing until just combined. Stir in the apple, then pour the batter into the prepared tin.

Bake for 45–50 minutes, or until a skewer comes out clean when inserted in the centre. Leave to cool in the tin for a few minutes, then invert onto a wire rack to cool completely. If you like, dust with icing sugar before serving.

NOTE: For ground almonds, if you don't wish to grind them yourself, you can simply purchase some almond meal, which is quite finely ground and will result in a refined, smooth texture. I like a slightly coarser texture, so I prefer to grind the nuts myself. To do so, simply place the required quantity in a mortar or food processor and grind to your desired texture.

There's a deli near my house where they place the just-delivered ricotta, still warm, on the counter in tubs. It's as fresh as fresh can be and, if I'm there, I cannot resist. Ricotta is so versatile and if I have any in the fridge – as I usually do – it will surely be used in something within a day or two. One of the nicest ways is in a cake. Pine nuts, while often only thought of for savoury dishes, are commonly used in Italian sweets – and they look beautiful, too, especially once covered in a dusting of icing sugar. This is a simple cake, ideal for leaving on the kitchen counter with a knife, so people can slice off pieces as the day passes.

PEAR, RICOTTA AND PINE NUT CAKE

SERVES 8–10

150 g unsalted butter, softened

150 g (⅔ cup) caster sugar

2 eggs

200 g fresh full-fat ricotta

1 vanilla pod, split and seeds scraped, or 1 teaspoon vanilla bean paste

finely grated zest of 2 lemons

250 g (1⅔ cups) self-raising flour, sifted

3 pears (about 500 g in total), peeled, cored and cut into 2 cm pieces

3 tablespoons pine nuts

icing sugar, for dusting

Preheat the oven to 180°C. Grease a 21 cm round cake tin with butter and line with baking paper.

Cream the butter and sugar together, either using a wooden spoon or a stand mixer fitted with a paddle attachment, until light and fluffy. Add the eggs, one at a time, beating well between each addition. Spoon in the ricotta, along with the vanilla and lemon zest. Add the flour and gently mix until the batter is smooth and the flour is well incorporated. Stir in the pear, then spoon the batter into the prepared tin. The batter will be quite stiff, so be as gentle as possible. Top with the pine nuts and bake for 45 minutes, or until a skewer comes out clean when inserted in the centre.

Leave to cool in the tin for a few minutes, then invert onto a wire rack to cool completely.

Lightly dust the cake with icing sugar before serving.

This recipe is inspired by the brownies at one of my favourite Tokyo cake shops, Sunday Bakeshop. The combination of chocolate and lemon may seem strange, but the slight acidity of the thin lemon slices pairs beautifully with the chocolate. Other toppings, such as raspberries, halved hazelnuts, or chopped macadamias or almonds, would all be great alternatives if you don't have any lemons on hand.

BROWNIES WITH LEMON

MAKES 9

100 g unsalted butter, softened

100 g brown sugar

200 g caster sugar

1 vanilla pod, split and seeds scraped, or 1 teaspoon vanilla bean paste

150 g (1 cup) plain flour

85 g (⅔ cup) unsweetened Dutch-process cocoa powder

pinch of sea salt

3 eggs, lightly beaten

100 g dark chocolate (70% cocoa), roughly chopped

9 very thin lemon slices

Preheat the oven to 180°C. Grease a 21 cm square cake tin with butter and line with baking paper.

Cream the butter, sugars and vanilla together, either using a wooden spoon or a stand mixer fitted with a paddle attachment, until pale and creamy. Sift in the flour and cocoa powder, add the salt and gently combine. Stir through the eggs and, once incorporated, fold in the chocolate. Spoon the batter into the prepared tin and arrange the lemon slices evenly over the surface.

Bake for 25–30 minutes. The edges should be just coming away from the sides while the middle should still be a little soft. Allow to cool briefly in the tin, then transfer to a wire rack to cool completely. Cut into squares to serve. The brownies will keep in an airtight container for up to 3 days, but they are best eaten not too long after cooling down.

A classic baked cheesecake is reliable and delicious. I top mine with whatever fruit is in season or leave it completely plain. Cheesecakes are very popular in our house and are often requested for birthdays, and I'm happy to oblige. Although you may feel the urge to bake this in a springform tin, do not. They are rarely watertight and you will be left with a soggy-bottomed cheesecake. A regular tin is fine and you'll find the cheesecake is sturdy enough, once chilled, to be flipped out onto a plate, then inverted again onto your serving plate.

CLASSIC BAKED CHEESECAKE

SERVES 8–10

750 g full-fat cream cheese, softened

400 g sour cream

125 g caster sugar

1 teaspoon vanilla extract

½ teaspoon ground cinnamon

finely grated zest of 1 lemon

3 eggs, lightly beaten

BISCUIT BASE

250 g Granita or other plain semi-sweet biscuits

1 tablespoon caster sugar

pinch of sea salt

½ teaspoon ground cinnamon

125 g unsalted butter, melted and cooled

Preheat the oven to 170°C.

To make the base, place the biscuits, sugar, salt and cinnamon in a food processor and blitz until you have a fine crumb. Tip the mixture into a bowl and pour over the melted butter. Mix to combine. Press the mixture evenly into the base of a 26 cm round cake tin (not springform) and bake for 10 minutes. Remove from the oven and place in a deep baking tray.

Meanwhile, mix together the cream cheese, sour cream, sugar, vanilla, cinnamon and lemon zest until very well combined. You can use a stand mixer fitted with a whisk attachment for ease. Gently mix in the egg until just combined. Pour the cheesecake mixture over the biscuit base, then fill the baking tray with enough boiling water to come halfway up the side of the cake tin. Carefully place in the oven and bake for 35–40 minutes until just set. The centre will still be wobbly, but will firm up as it cools. If you want, you can continue to cook the cheesecake a little longer, until it really puffs up and colours – this will give you an entirely different cake, more like the style of cheesecake you'd find in Spain. It will be less creamy and have more texture.

Allow the cheesecake to cool to room temperature, then refrigerate for at least 4 hours. When ready to serve, run a sharp knife around the edge of the tin and invert the cheesecake onto a flat board or plate, then flip back onto a serving plate or cake stand. To help release the cheesecake, I usually sit the tin in hot water for 30 seconds, or warm with a kitchen blowtorch or carefully over a gas stovetop. This will melt the butter in the base ever so slightly. Top with your choice of fruit.

A banana cake dressed up with zingy lemon icing is the kind of cake I remember eating at school fetes as a young girl. This one is very moist and the coconut adds a great texture, too. While, of course, it doesn't necessarily *need* the icing, it is a lovely addition.

BANANA AND COCONUT CAKE WITH LEMON ICING

SERVES 8–10

3 eggs

100 g caster sugar

50 g brown sugar

1 vanilla pod, split and seeds scraped, or 1 teaspoon vanilla bean paste

150 ml olive or neutral vegetable oil

60 g (1 cup) shredded coconut, plus extra for sprinkling

270 g self-raising flour, sifted

3 mashed ripe bananas (around 300 g in total)

200 ml buttermilk

LEMON ICING

finely grated zest and juice of 1 lemon

250 g (2 cups) icing sugar, sifted, plus extra if needed

Preheat the oven to 180°C. Grease a 21 cm round cake tin with butter and line with baking paper.

In a large bowl, whisk the eggs and sugars together until pale and light. Add the vanilla and drizzle in the oil, whisking to combine. Alternately and in small batches, add the shredded coconut, flour, banana and buttermilk, mixing well between each addition. Pour the batter into the prepared tin and bake for 50–60 minutes, or until a skewer comes out clean when inserted in the centre. Leave to cool in the tin for a few minutes, then invert onto a wire rack to cool completely.

For the icing, combine the lemon zest and juice with the icing sugar, whisking until smooth. The icing should be runny enough to pour but thick enough to cover the cake. Add more sugar to thicken if you need to. Pour the icing over the cake and generously scatter with extra shredded coconut.

A throw-it-all-together cookie I made while baking with my son, Haruki, one morning. Pouring with rain outside, we kept ourselves busy in the kitchen. We added all of our favourite things and ended up with a delicious batch of chewy cookies. A few weeks later, with those cookies still on my mind, I set out to make them again, this time with measurements and timings and less mess (although part of me loves Haruki's baking mess). These cookies are perfect for dunking into a cold glass of milk, no matter what your age. If you want to make them even more decadent, place a few pieces of chopped chocolate on the tops of the cookies half way through the cooking time. Once the cookie dough has been made and rolled into balls, they can be stored in the freezer and then popped in the oven at a moment's notice – just increase the cooking time by a few minutes.

DARK CHOCOLATE, WALNUT AND OAT COOKIES

MAKES ABOUT 27

250 g unsalted butter, softened

150 g caster sugar

100 g brown sugar

1 egg, lightly beaten

1 teaspoon vanilla extract

275 g plain flour

½ teaspoon baking powder

pinch of sea salt, plus extra for sprinkling

60 g rolled oats

150 g dark chocolate (70% cocoa), roughly chopped

70 g walnuts, roughly chopped

Cream the butter and sugars together, either using a wooden spoon or a stand mixer fitted with a paddle attachment, until pale and very fluffy. Add the egg and vanilla and continue to mix until well incorporated. Sift in the flour and baking powder, add the salt and gently mix until everything is well incorporated (but be careful not to over-mix). Now mix in the rolled oats, dark chocolate and walnuts. Cover the bowl and chill in the fridge for 30–60 minutes to to firm up.

Preheat the oven to 180°C and line four baking trays with baking paper.

Roll heaped tablespoons of the dough into balls (about 40 g each) and place on the trays, leaving room for the cookies to spread. If you only have one or two trays, keep the dough in the fridge while each batch is cooking and then repeat the process once you have a free tray.

Bake for 12–14 minutes until lightly golden. Sprinkle with a little sea salt and then allow to cool slightly before transferring to a wire rack to cool completely. The cookies will keep in an airtight container for up to a week.

SPRING

The first broad beans of the season, young and tender, remind me of sitting with my
grandmother, podding what seemed like a mountain of them. The beans would then
be dried and stored in large jars to use over the coming months. There are many
ingredients that bring out these vivid snapshots of time from my mind. Whenever
I see blossoms beginning to burst from cherry or stone-fruit trees in my neighbourhood,
I'm immediately transported to the Japanese countryside, where I have enjoyed many
springs. When the trees are in full bloom, and they are for only a day or two, the beauty
is incomparable; and in the days that follow, the ground is carpeted in petals, declaring
the fleeting nature of the seasons. After a long winter, the fresh and vibrant produce
that begins to show itself is a gift to savour. What a wonderful time.

While it took me a few trips to Japan to appreciate *shokupan* – fluffy white and incredibly soft bread – I am now a fully-fledged convert and seek out thick slices of the stuff at any cafe or bakery we go to. Sometimes with melted cheese and honey, as I ate in Kyoto, served with a boiled egg and black coffee, as they do in Nagoya, or as a sandwich to eat on the bullet train. However it's served, it is so delicious and nostalgic. A hotel we like to stay at in Tokyo is famous for its French toast. In fact, even if you are a guest and plan to eat at the cafe for breakfast, you must book in specifically for the French toast. The thick slices of shokupan are soaked in a fairly traditional mixture of eggs, milk and some flavourings. The secret is that they are soaked overnight in the egg bath. Served simply with seasonal fruits, a dusting of icing sugar and a drizzle of maple syrup, it is the best French toast I have ever eaten. And while it can be found all over Japan, I still associate it with Tokyo, hence the name of this recipe. Because shokupan (or Japanese milk bread) is still a little difficult to come by outside of Japan, regular white bread, brioche or challah are fine substitutes.

TOKYO-STYLE FRENCH TOAST

SERVES 4

5 eggs

300 ml full-cream milk

1 teaspoon vanilla extract

3 tablespoons caster sugar, plus extra for sprinkling

4 x 4 cm thick slices of shokupan, white bread, brioche or challah

100 g unsalted butter, plus extra to serve

2 tablespoons extra-virgin olive oil

maple syrup, to serve

strawberries or other fruit of your choice, to serve

A full day before you plan on eating, whisk together the eggs, milk, vanilla and sugar in a large bowl.

Arrange the slices of bread in a deep tray where they fit snugly and pour the egg mixture over the top. Cover and refrigerate for 24 hours, flipping halfway. This stage is really important and can't be short cut.

Preheat the oven to 150°C and line a baking tray with baking paper.

Sprinkle each slice of soaked bread with a little extra sugar on both sides.

Heat half of the butter and olive oil in a large frying pan over a medium–high heat. When the butter is foaming, place two of the slices in the pan and cook for around 3 minutes on each side until golden. Transfer to the prepared tray and keep warm in the oven. Repeat with the remaining butter, oil and bread.

Serve the French toast with extra butter, maple syrup and fresh fruit.

This is a perfect brunch recipe, but also makes an equally satisfying light lunch or dinner. Be sure to choose a starchy potato for best results.

POTATO PANCAKES WITH HERBED SOUR CREAM AND SMOKED TROUT

SERVES 4

750 g desiree or other starchy potatoes, grated

1 onion, grated

1 tablespoon plain flour

1 egg, lightly beaten

sea salt and black pepper

ghee or olive oil, for frying

4 soft-boiled eggs, halved

small handful of snow pea shoots or rocket

350 g hot-smoked rainbow trout, skin and bones removed and flesh flaked

1 lemon, sliced

HERBED SOUR CREAM

200 g sour cream

handful of finely chopped dill fronds

handful of finely chopped chives

1 tablespoon extra-virgin olive oil

1 tablespoon lemon juice

pinch of sea salt

For the herbed sour cream, simply combine all of the ingredients in a small bowl. Set aside in the fridge while you work on the pancakes.

Place the grated potato in a large bowl. Cover with cold water and agitate with your hands. Drain well then squeeze out any excess moisture and place in a clean dry bowl. Add the onion, flour, egg and a good pinch each of salt and pepper. Mix well, using your hands to really work the mixture together for a few minutes. This helps the starch come out of the potatoes, which will hold the pancakes together without having to add too much flour or egg. You should see the mixture change and come together as you do this.

Heat 1 tablespoon of ghee or oil in a large frying pan over a medium heat. Using a ¼ cup measurement, drop portions of the mixture into the pan and flatten them slightly using a spatula. Cook for about 5 minutes, flipping halfway, until golden, adding extra ghee or oil as needed. The mixture should make about 16 pancakes – it's best to cook them in batches so you don't overcrowd the pan. Drain the pancakes on paper towel and serve with the herbed sour cream, soft-boiled eggs, greens, trout and lemon.

Bigilla is a Maltese dip made with dried broad beans and lots of garlic. We used to dry our own broad beans when I was younger, as they weren't readily available and we needed to ensure we had a good supply until the following spring. I wanted to recreate the dip but using fresh broad beans, which are around for such a short time. You often need to double pod broad beans – first removing them from the outer pod where they rest and then peeling off the fibrous skin – leaving just the vibrant green and tender beans. Here, however, there is no need to double pod. Simply remove them from the pod, blanch and blitz. The skin gives necessary texture and structure to this dip, which I like to serve on crostini with ricotta.

NEW BIGILLA CROSTINI

SERVES 6–8 AS A SNACK

1 baguette, thinly sliced

extra-virgin olive oil, for drizzling

sea salt and black pepper

150 g fresh full-fat ricotta

NEW BIGILLA

1 kg broad beans, podded (you'll end up with about 400 g beans)

1 garlic clove, roughly chopped

juice of ½ lemon

handful of parsley, leaves picked

handful of mint, leaves picked

60–100 ml extra-virgin olive oil

sea salt

Preheat the oven to 180°C. Line two baking trays with baking paper.

To make the bigilla, blanch the podded broad beans in a saucepan of boiling water for 3–4 minutes until tender. How much time they need will depend on their size – young ones will take not much time at all. Drain and refresh in cold water. Place the beans in a small food processor along with the garlic, lemon and herbs. Process for 2 minutes until fairly smooth. Stream in enough olive oil to create a smooth, spoonable dip. Season to taste. Transfer to a serving bowl and set aside. Refrigerate if not using immediately.

Arrange the baguette slices on a tray and drizzle a little olive oil over each slice. Sprinkle with a generous amount of salt and bake for 8–10 minutes, or until golden. Set aside to cool.

Spread the baguette pieces with the broad bean dip and top with some ricotta. Drizzle with olive oil, season with salt and pepper and serve.

A simple recipe for the way I make my mum's chicken sandwiches, which I think she's served at every important event or party since I can remember. There is something so comfortably predictable about these sandwiches, which I love. If I have leftover roast chicken, I use this instead of the poached chicken breasts.

MUM'S CHICKEN SANDWICHES

SERVES 4

2 skinless chicken breast fillets (about 500 g in total)

3 peppercorns

1 fresh bay leaf

80 g mayonnaise (see page 51; omit the preserved lemon)

60 g crème fraîche

3 tablespoons finely chopped chives

small handful of parsley leaves, finely chopped

1 teaspoon dijon mustard

50 g (⅓ cup) toasted almonds, roughly chopped

2 celery stalks, finely chopped

1 tablespoon salted capers, rinsed and roughly chopped

sea salt and black pepper

8 slices of good-quality sourdough bread

extra-virgin olive oil, for brushing and drizzling

handful of rocket or cos lettuce

Place the chicken breasts in a small saucepan with the peppercorns and bay leaf. Cover with cold water and bring to the boil over a high heat, then immediately reduce the heat to low and simmer for around 10 minutes until just cooked through. Allow to cool in the broth.

Finely chop the chicken and place in a large bowl. Add the mayonnaise, crème fraîche, herbs, mustard, almonds, celery and capers, season well with salt and pepper and mix so that everything is well combined.

Brush the slices of bread with olive oil, spoon some chicken filling onto each slice and top with some rocket or lettuce. Sandwich with the remaining bread slices, cut in half and serve drizzled with some more olive oil.

We make these sandwiches for birthday parties or larger gatherings and they are so popular they disappear in a flash. In Japan, unused sandwich crusts are often made into sweet rusks by frying them in the hot oil (before the chicken, to avoid any chance of mixing flavours), then tossing them in cinnamon sugar. This is how my husband, Nori, remembers it from his childhood. The chicken recipe below can be used to make karaage on its own – simply cut the chicken into smaller pieces before marinating and then proceed as usual. Serve on rice or by itself with a good dollop of Kewpie for dipping.

CHICKEN KARAAGE SANDWICHES

SERVES 4

500 g chicken thigh fillets, large thighs halved

200 g white cabbage, finely shredded

2 spring onions, finely sliced

2 tablespoons extra-virgin olive oil

juice of ½ lemon

sea salt and black pepper

vegetable oil, for deep-frying

potato starch, for coating

hot English or Japanese mustard, for spreading

8 slices of shokupan (see Note) or white bread, crusts removed

100 g Kewpie mayonnaise (see Note)

KARAAGE MARINADE

2 garlic cloves, grated

1 cm piece of ginger, grated

1 tablespoon sesame oil

2 tablespoons soy sauce

1 tablespoon mirin

3 tablespoons saké

1 teaspoon brown sugar

1 egg, lightly beaten

1 tablespoon potato starch

Using a fork, poke holes in the chicken to better allow the marinade to soak in. Place the chicken in a shallow container so it fits snugly. Whisk the marinade ingredients in a bowl and pour over the chicken. Use your hands to turn the chicken in the marinade so it's well coated. Cover and set aside in the fridge to marinate for 30–60 minutes.

Meanwhile, combine the cabbage, spring onion, olive oil and lemon juice in a large bowl, season well and set aside.

Pour the vegetable oil into a heavy-based saucepan or wok to a depth of 5 cm. Heat the oil to 170°C, or hot enough that a cube of bread dropped into the oil turns golden brown in 20 seconds.

Shake the excess marinade from the chicken, then toss the chicken in potato starch to coat. Fry, in batches, for 4 minutes or until cooked through and golden. Remove with a slotted spoon and drain on a wire rack.

Spread a thin layer of mustard on four of the bread slices and a generous layer of mayo on the others. Place a piece of chicken on the mustard, top with some slaw, then sandwich with the remaining slices of bread. Cut each sandwich in half and serve.

NOTES: Here, I've used the traditional Japanese milk bread called *shokupan*, which is incredibly fluffy. Regular white bread is fine, too.

You can also use the mayonnaise on page 51; just omit the preserved lemon.

While not a traditional way to eat soba noodles, soba salad is one of my lunchtime staples. I vary the ingredients depending on what I feel like or what is available. Soba noodles are made from buckwheat or a combination of buckwheat and wheat, the latter being more common. Broad beans can be used instead of the edamame and often I'll add cherry tomatoes and avocado, too.

SOBA SALAD

SERVES 4

300 g frozen edamame beans

handful of greens, such as mizuna, mustard greens or rocket

400 g soba noodles

GINGER–SESAME DRESSING

3 tablespoons soy sauce

2 tablespoons mirin

2 tablespoons rice wine vinegar

2 tablespoons tahini

2 tablespoons sesame oil

2 cm piece of ginger, finely grated

1 teaspoon caster sugar

sea salt

TO SERVE

shredded nori

toasted black and white sesame seeds

shichimi togarashi

finely sliced spring onion

Blanch the edamame in a saucepan of boiling water over a high heat for 1–2 minutes, or cook according to the packet instructions. Remove with a slotted spoon (don't drain the pan as you'll use the water to cook the noodles) and rinse with cold water to stop the cooking process. Drain, then place in a large bowl along with the greens.

Add the soba noodles to the pan of boiling water and cook until al dente, according to the packet instructions (it should be around 6 minutes). Drain and rinse under cold running water. Leave to drain for a minute or two, then add to the edamame and greens.

Meanwhile, place all the ingredients for the dressing in a small jug and whisk until combined. Season to taste and adjust to suit – feel free to add more of any of the dressing ingredients to your liking. Pour over the noodle mixture and toss until well coated.

Divide among bowls and top with the nori, sesame seeds, shichimi togarashi and spring onion.

Broad beans and pecorino are a classic combination. Bring in the mint and it's spring on a plate. If you want to make this salad more substantial, you could add a grain such as farro or some soft-boiled eggs.

BROAD BEAN SALAD WITH MINT AND PECORINO

SERVES 4

1.2 kg broad beans, podded (you'll end up with about 480 g)

iced water, for refreshing

large handful of mint leaves

large handful of parsley leaves

40 g pecorino, shaved

3 tablespoons extra-virgin olive oil

juice of 1 lemon

sea salt

Blanch the broad beans in a large saucepan of boiling water for 2–3 minutes until tender, then drain and refresh in an ice bath. Pop the broad beans out of their jackets, discarding the skins, and place in a bowl. Toss with the herbs and pecorino.

In a small bowl, whisk the olive oil with the lemon juice and season with a generous pinch of salt. Pour over the salad and serve.

Runner beans, also known as Roman beans or flat beans, are wonderful during springtime and into summer. They should be crispy and bright, and are great in soups and stews. I also love cooking these beans in a hot pan so they become charred and smoky.

RUNNER BEAN SALAD WITH FRIED ALMONDS

SERVES 4

800 g runner beans, trimmed and cut into 5 cm lengths

2 tablespoons extra-virgin olive oil

sea salt

HERBED SOUR CREAM DRESSING

200 g sour cream

large handful of dill fronds, finely chopped

large handful of mint leaves, finely chopped

juice of 1 lemon

3 tablespoons extra-virgin olive oil

1 small red onion, finely chopped

pinch of sea salt

FRIED ALMONDS

155 g (1 cup) almonds

2 tablespoons extra-virgin olive oil

sea salt

1 teaspoon smoked paprika

Place the beans in a large bowl. Pour over the olive oil and season generously with salt. Mix so that all the beans are well coated. Heat a large frying pan over a high heat and cook the beans, in batches, until they are just cooked through and a little coloured. Return to the bowl and set aside to cool slightly.

Meanwhile, mix together all of the dressing ingredients in a small bowl. Spoon over the warm beans and mix well.

For the fried almonds, mix the almonds in a small bowl with the olive oil and a generous sprinkling of salt. Heat a small frying pan over a high heat and fry the almonds, stirring continuously, for around 2 minutes. Add the paprika and fry for another 1 minute until the almonds are toasted and fragrant.

Scatter the almonds over the beans and serve.

This is one of my favourite salads to make – it uses cavolo nero as a base and is built up with croutons, apple, mint and celery. The real highlight, though, is the parmesan dressing, which is so full of flavour and creamy without weighing everything down.

CAVOLO NERO, APPLE AND MINT SALAD

SERVES 4

½ bunch of cavolo nero (about 150 g), tough stems removed, leaves washed thoroughly and roughly chopped

3 tablespoons extra-virgin olive oil

sea salt

2 slices of sourdough bread, torn into large croutons

60 g almonds

1 pink lady apple, halved, cored and finely sliced

1 celery stalk, finely sliced

handful of mint leaves, torn

PARMESAN DRESSING

40 g parmesan, finely grated

3 tablespoons extra-virgin olive oil

finely grated zest and juice of 1 lemon

1 small garlic clove, grated

sea salt and black pepper

Preheat the oven to 180°C.

Place the cavolo nero in a large bowl and pour over half of the olive oil. Season well with salt and massage into the leaves. Set aside.

In another bowl, toss the croutons in the remaining olive oil and season with salt. Arrange on a baking tray and toast for 15 minutes, or until golden. Add the almonds to the tray for the final 5 minutes. Remove from the oven, then lightly crush the croutons using a rolling pin and roughly chop the almonds. Add these to the bowl with the kale, followed by the apple, celery and mint.

For the dressing, place all the ingredients in a small food processor and blitz for about 1 minute until smooth and creamy. Alternatively, simply whisk everything together. Pour the dressing over the salad and toss well using your hands.

A light salad that has a little of everything – bitterness, sourness, crunch and sweetness. It is perfect for outdoor eating and one of my go-tos when the warmer weather arrives. Sometimes I swap the prawns for poached chicken breast if that's what I have on hand, which works really well. Pomelo is a great alternative to the grapefruit, too, if you happen to find some at the market or grocer.

GRAPEFRUIT AND PRAWN SALAD

SERVES 4

16 peeled, deveined cooked prawns (about 800 g unpeeled, 350 g peeled)

1 pink grapefruit, peeled and segmented

1 long green chilli, finely sliced

1 bunch of mint, leaves picked

large handful of coriander, leaves picked

2 Lebanese cucumbers, peeled and cut on the diagonal into 5 mm thick slices

50 g toasted shredded coconut, plus extra to serve

60 g roasted peanuts, plus extra to serve

SWEET AND SOUR DRESSING

2 teaspoons caster sugar, plus extra if needed

juice of 2 limes, plus extra if needed

2 tablespoons fish sauce, plus extra if needed

For the dressing, whisk together the ingredients in small bowl and taste. It should be a nice balance of sweet, sour and salty. Add more of any of the ingredients to achieve the correct balance.

Place the prawns, grapefruit, chilli, herbs, cucumber, coconut and peanuts in a large bowl. Pour over the dressing and toss gently.

Arrange the salad on a large serving plate. Scatter over the extra peanuts and coconut and serve immediately.

This is such a traditional dish and, in my opinion, should be kept as simple as possible. The key is really good-quality ingredients and getting the timing just right. I like to get the water on the boil and allow it to bubble away while I begin the sauce – this means that as the sauce simmers, the pasta can be plunged into the boiling salty water without delay. There are countless variations of this dish, but even adding basil, as I've done here, isn't exactly true to its origins. A friend, who happens to be a wonderful cook from Amatrice, suggests this addition, and it does add a little freshness, which I love. Amatriciana is most commonly served with bucatini, but spaghetti or a dried short pasta like rigatoni are also great. Although it's tempting to just substitute the harder-to-find guanciale with pancetta, the sweet, salty, peppery flavour that guanciale brings cannot be beaten.

BUCATINI ALL'AMATRICIANA

SERVES 4

150 g guanciale, rind removed, cut into 1 cm lardons

400 g canned whole peeled tomatoes

1 dried red chilli

320 g dried bucatini

60 g (⅔ cup) finely grated pecorino, plus extra to serve

basil leaves, to serve (optional)

Bring a large saucepan of water to the boil over a high heat while you make the sauce.

Place the guanciale in a large frying pan over a low heat and fry gently, stirring occasionally, until most of the fat has rendered out and the guanciale is lightly golden. Increase the heat to medium and add the tomatoes, pressing them with the back of a wooden spoon to break them up. Crumble in the chilli and simmer for 8–10 minutes, or until the sauce is thick.

While the sauce is simmering away, generously season the boiling water with salt and cook the pasta for a minute or two less than the packet instructions until just under al dente.

Now, it's a matter of timing. You want the sauce and pasta to be ready at the same time.

Remove the sauce from the heat and scatter in the cheese, stirring to melt it into the sauce. Drain the pasta, reserving 250 ml (1 cup) of the cooking water. Transfer the bucatini to the sauce along with most of the cooking water and stir over a medium heat for 2 minutes to ensure everything is well coated and the pasta is al dente. If the sauce begins to look dry, add the remaining cooking water. Scatter over some extra pecorino and the basil leaves, if using, and serve. You shouldn't need to add any salt or pepper as the guanciale will season the dish perfectly.

Malfatti, meaning 'badly made', refers to the rustic nature of these dumplings. I shape them in a wine glass for ease, as suggested by the inimitable Rose Gray and Ruth Rogers of The River Café. It really works and is by far the easiest and least messy way to roll them. I use buffalo ricotta as it is very creamy and I adore the flavour, however another firm full-fat ricotta can be used instead. If the ricotta you are using is a little wet, simply drain it in a sieve for 30 minutes or overnight to remove excess liquid.

SILVERBEET AND RICOTTA MALFATTI WITH BROWN BUTTER SAUCE

SERVES 4–6

1 kg silverbeet, tough stems removed

500 g buffalo ricotta

100 g (1 cup) grated parmesan, plus extra to serve

3 eggs, lightly beaten

pinch of freshly grated nutmeg

sea salt and black pepper

3 tablespoons tipo 00 or plain flour

semolina flour, for dusting (see page 12)

125 g lightly salted butter

12 sage leaves

Blanch the silverbeet in salted boiling water for around 1 minute until wilted. Drain and, when cool enough to handle, squeeze out any excess water. Finely chop the cooked leaves and combine with the ricotta in a large bowl. Add the parmesan, egg and nutmeg and season generously with salt and pepper. Gently fold in the tipo 00 or plain flour, then leave to set in the fridge for 30 minutes.

Roll the mixture into walnut-sized balls and coat well in semolina flour. I find the easiest way to do this is by dropping a spoonful of mixture into a well-floured wine glass and swirling it around as you would before taking a sip. The swirling motion creates a perfect sphere, which can then be tipped onto a tray of semolina flour to coat. Transfer the tray to the fridge for at least 1 hour to allow the malfatti to firm up.

Bring a large saucepan of salted water to the boil. Reduce to a gentle simmer, add the malfatti and cook for 2–3 minutes until they float to the surface. Drain and transfer to a warm serving dish.

Meanwhile, melt the butter in a small frying pan over a high heat. Once foaming, add the sage leaves and stir constantly until the leaves are crispy and the butter has browned. Pour the browned butter and sage over the malfatti and top with a good scattering of grated parmesan.

This is probably my favourite soup to make. Without all the toppings, it's delicious, but with the addition of the fried onion, soft egg and harissa, it really is something else – full of wonderful textures and punchy flavours.

LENTIL SOUP WITH FRIED ONION AND SOFT EGGS

100 g dried chickpeas or 400 g canned chickpeas, rinsed and drained

3 tablespoons extra-virgin olive oil

1 onion, finely diced

3 garlic cloves, roughly chopped

1 celery stalk, finely diced

1 small carrot, finely diced

2 cm piece of ginger, finely chopped

½ teaspoon ground turmeric

1 teaspoon coriander seeds, freshly ground

1 teaspoon cumin seeds, freshly ground

½ teaspoon ground ginger

pinch of dried chilli

400 g canned whole peeled tomatoes

300 g (1½ cups) puy lentils, rinsed

2 litres chicken or vegetable stock

½ bunch of coriander, leaves and stalks finely chopped

juice of 1 lemon

sea salt

FRIED ONION

20 g butter

1 tablespoon extra-virgin olive oil

½ teaspoon cumin seeds, freshly ground

1 onion, finely sliced

sea salt

POACHED EGGS

1 tablespoon white vinegar

4 very fresh eggs

TO SERVE

plain full-fat yoghurt

harissa paste

chopped coriander leaves

If using dried chickpeas, place in a bowl, cover with cold water and leave to soak overnight. Drain, then cook in boiling water for about 40 minutes until tender. Drain again.

Warm the olive oil in a large heavy-based saucepan over a low–medium heat. Gently fry the onion, garlic, celery, carrot and fresh ginger, stirring occasionally, for around 15 minutes until softened and beginning to colour.

Increase the heat to medium and add the turmeric, coriander, cumin, ground ginger and dried chilli. Stir so that everything is well coated in the spices and fry for 2–3 minutes until fragrant. Add the tomatoes, breaking them up with the back of a wooden spoon, followed by the lentils and the stock or water. Simmer, half covered, for 30 minutes, or until the lentils are almost cooked. Add the chickpeas and continue to simmer for a further 10 minutes. Stir through the coriander and lemon juice, season to taste and keep warm.

Meanwhile, for the fried onion, heat the butter and olive oil in a frying pan over a medium–high heat. Add the cumin and onion and fry for 5–8 minutes, stirring regularly, until the onion is crispy and golden. Season with salt.

To poach the eggs, heat a large saucepan of water over a low heat and, when just simmering, add the vinegar. Make a whirlpool in the water using a wooden spoon and add the eggs. It's best to crack each egg into a cup so you can gently slide them into the water. Poach for about 3 minutes until just cooked. Remove the poached eggs with a slotted spoon and place them on a plate lined with paper towel to absorb any excess water.

Ladle the soup into serving bowls and top each with a poached egg, some fried onion, dollops of plain yoghurt and harissa paste and a scattering of coriander.

Perfect for a long lunch with friends, this lamb is zingy and so tender thanks to the long cooking time. I love adding lots of herbs to the tabbouleh – the lamb is quite rich, so this freshness is a welcome accompaniment.

LAMB SHOULDER WITH TABBOULEH

SERVES 6–8

1 x 2 kg bone-in lamb shoulder

1 tablespoon cumin seeds, toasted

1 tablespoon coriander seeds, toasted

sea salt

1 teaspoon sumac

finely grated zest of 1 lemon

2 tablespoons extra-virgin olive oil

100 ml dry white wine

TABBOULEH

20 g unsalted butter

100 ml extra-virgin olive oil

100 g coarse burghul

200 ml hot water or chicken or vegetable stock

sea salt

80 g pitted green olives, roughly chopped

bunch of mint, leaves picked and roughly chopped

bunch of parsley, leaves picked and roughly chopped

½ bunch of coriander, leaves picked and roughly chopped

seeds of 1 pomegranate

50 g sultanas or currants

50 g (⅓ cup) toasted almonds, roughly chopped

juice of 1 lemon

Preheat the oven to 150°C.

Place the lamb in a deep baking tray so it fits nice and snug.

Roughly grind the cumin and coriander seeds with a large pinch of salt using a mortar and pestle. Add the sumac, lemon zest and olive oil and stir to combine. Rub all over the lamb so it's well covered. Pour the wine into the tray along with enough water to fill to a depth of about 1 cm. Cover the lamb with a layer of baking paper and then a layer of foil and roast for 5 hours, or until the meat is falling apart and tender.

Increase the oven temperature to 180°C, remove the foil and roast the lamb for a further 30 minutes, or until golden and crisp.

Meanwhile, for the tabbouleh, heat the butter and 2 tablespoons of the olive oil in a large heavy-based saucepan over a medium heat. Add the burghul and stir well to coat all of the grains. Toast the burghul for 1 minute, stirring continuously so the grains don't burn. Add the hot water or stock and a pinch of salt and bring to the boil. Reduce the heat to low, cover with a lid and cook for about 5 minutes, or until all of the liquid has been absorbed. Keep covered and leave to sit for 10 minutes. (If you are using finer burghul, be sure to check the packet instructions as cooking times may vary.) Transfer the cooked burghul to a large bowl along with the olives, herbs, fruit and almonds. Whisk the lemon juice and the remaining 3 tablespoons of olive oil together in a small bowl, season with salt and pour over the salad. Toss to combine.

Pull the lamb apart and serve with the tabbouleh.

My good friend Jessilla, who also happened to be my flatmate during my university days, would always tear out recipes from the weekend newspaper lift-outs and stick them to our fridge if she thought them worthy of being cooked in our Carlton share house. I always appreciated how analogue this was and can still remember one of the recipes that made it on there. It was a lamb and green bean stew made with flat beans. Here is my version. I have successfully made this with lamb chops, too. Be sure the meat you buy isn't too lean as some fat is essential to keep it tender.

LAMB AND GREEN BEAN STEW

SERVES 4–6

1 kg boneless lamb shoulder, cut into 3 cm pieces

sea salt

2 tablespoons extra-virgin olive oil, plus extra for drizzling

2 onions, roughly chopped

125 ml (½ cup) dry white wine

400 g canned whole peeled tomatoes

500 g green beans, trimmed

large handful of dill fronds, roughly chopped, plus extra to serve

large handful of coriander leaves, roughly chopped

plain full-fat yoghurt, to serve

Season the lamb generously with salt.

Heat the olive oil in a large heavy-based saucepan or cast-iron pot with a lid over a medium–high heat. Sear the lamb on all sides until golden, cooking in batches if necessary. Remove from the pan and set aside. Reduce the heat to low–medium and cook the onion for about 10 minutes until soft and just beginning to colour. Pour in the white wine, scraping any brown bits from the bottom of the pan. Return the lamb to the pan along with the tomatoes and 1 tomato can (400 ml) of water. Cover with a lid and cook for around 2 hours, stirring occasionally, until the lamb is tender.

Add the beans and cook, uncovered, for another 30 minutes. Stir through the herbs, check for seasoning and serve with a large spoonful of plain yoghurt, some extra dill and an extra drizzle of olive oil.

There are countless variations of hunter's stew, known as *Pollo alla cacciatora* – some *in bianco* (without tomatoes), some without olives or with different herbs or aromatics. Mine is a very simple one, with tomatoes, large green olives and fragrant rosemary and bay. It is a straightforward dish that is even better the next day. Serve it on a bed of soft polenta or simply with bread to mop up the juices.

HUNTER'S CHICKEN STEW

SERVES 4–6

1 x 1.2 kg chicken, cut into 8 pieces

sea salt

100 g (⅔ cup) plain flour

2 tablespoons extra-virgin olive oil

20 g unsalted butter

1 onion, roughly chopped

1 celery stalk, finely chopped

3 garlic cloves, finely chopped

125 ml (½ cup) dry white wine

1 rosemary sprig

1 fresh bay leaf

400 g canned whole peeled tomatoes

250 ml (1 cup) chicken stock

100 g whole green olives

Season the chicken with salt, then dredge lightly in the flour, shaking off any excess.

Heat the olive oil and butter in a large heavy-based saucepan or cast-iron pot over a medium heat and brown the chicken in batches until golden on all sides. Set aside.

Reduce the heat to low and add the onion and celery. Gently fry for around 10 minutes and, when beginning to turn golden, add the garlic and cook for a further minute. Pour in the wine, scraping up any brown bits left over from frying the chicken. Add the rosemary, bay leaf, tomatoes and chicken stock and break up the tomatoes with the back of a wooden spoon. Increase the heat to medium and, when beginning to simmer, return the chicken to the pan, nestling it into the liquid. Simmer over a medium–low heat for 25 minutes, or until the chicken is tender and the stew has thickened. Scatter over the olives and cook for a few minutes more, then season to taste and serve.

This is my back-pocket recipe for a butter cake that can be adapted to suit the seasons. Most fruits are a lovely addition, gently pressed into the batter – just be mindful of the cooking time. Fruits like apple or quince are better when cooked prior to adding, whereas rhubarb, blueberries or blackberries can be used as the raspberries are here. This cake is based on a traditional French cake called the *quatre quarts* or 'four quarters' cake, as it uses just four ingredients – all the same weight – to form the basic batter.

SIMPLE BUTTER CAKE WITH RASPBERRIES

SERVES 8

3 eggs

200 g caster sugar

1 vanilla pod, split and seeds scraped, or 1 teaspoon vanilla bean paste

200 g unsalted butter, melted and cooled

200 g (1⅓ cups) self-raising flour

125 g raspberries

icing sugar, for dusting

Preheat the oven to 180°C. Grease a 21 cm square cake tin with butter and line with baking paper.

Beat the eggs with the sugar for 3–4 minutes, or until very pale and fluffy. This is best done in a stand mixer fitted with a paddle attachment. Add the vanilla, then the butter and mix until well combined. Sift in the flour and gently stir until well incorporated.

Pour into the prepared tin and bake for 15 minutes. Remove the tin from the oven and gently press the raspberries on top of the batter – adding them at this later stage stops all the fruit from sinking to the bottom of the cake. Cook for another 25–30 minutes until a skewer comes out clean when inserted in the centre. Leave to cool in the tin for a few minutes, then invert onto a wire rack to cool completely.

Lightly dust the cake with icing sugar before serving.

Roasting strawberries is a wonderful way to bring out their sweetness. They also turn a deep crimson, which looks beautiful in contrast to the snowy white peaks of the crème fraîche. This pastry is really decadent and flaky and well worth making yourself. The great thing about this tart is that all of the elements can be prepared the day before and assembled just before serving, making it perfect for a spring picnic or gathering.

ROASTED STRAWBERRY AND CRÈME FRAÎCHE TART

SERVES 8

300 g (2 cups) plain flour, plus extra for dusting

1 tablespoon caster sugar

fine sea salt

200 g chilled unsalted butter, cut into cubes

1 egg yolk

1½–2½ tablespoons iced water

ROASTED STRAWBERRIES

500 g strawberries, hulled and halved, plus extra to serve

2 tarragon sprigs, plus extra to serve

3 tablespoons caster sugar

1 vanilla pod, split and seeds scraped

CANDIED ALMONDS

60 g toasted almonds

80 g caster sugar

ALMOND CREAM

200 g mascarpone

200 g crème fraîche

200 g fresh full-fat ricotta

1 vanilla pod, split and seeds scraped

½ teaspoon almond extract

60 g (½ cup) icing sugar, sifted

Combine the flour, sugar and a pinch of salt on a clean work surface. Rub the butter into the flour mixture using your fingertips until you have the texture of coarse breadcrumbs. Some larger pieces of butter are good, too. Mix in the egg yolk and sprinkle in enough iced water so that the dough just comes together. Flatten into a disc, wrap and refrigerate for 1 hour.

Preheat the oven to 180°C.

Take the pastry out of the fridge 10 minutes before you want to use it. Roll out on a lightly floured work surface to about 5 mm thick. Drape into a 23 cm loose-bottomed fluted tart tin, gently pressing into the edges. Trim any excess overhanging pastry, line with baking paper and fill with baking weights, dried beans or rice. Bake for 15 minutes. Remove the paper and weights and return to the oven for a further 15 minutes, or until the pastry is golden. Allow the pastry shell to cool completely before removing it from the tin.

For the roasted strawberries, keep the oven at 180°C and line a baking tray with baking paper. Place the strawberries in a bowl with the tarragon, sugar and vanilla and toss to coat. Arrange the strawberries on the baking tray in a single layer and roast for 30 minutes, or until they have released some juice and are a little softened. Set aside to cool.

For the candied almonds, line a baking tray with baking paper and grease the baking paper with olive oil. Place the almonds on the tray so they're nice and close together. Melt the sugar in a small saucepan over a low–medium heat, swirling the pan, for 5–7 minutes until it turns a deep amber colour. Pour the caramel over the almonds and allow to cool. Chop the candied almonds into small pieces and set aside.

For the almond cream, whip the mascarpone, crème fraîche and ricotta to stiff peaks in a large bowl. Stir through the remaining ingredients and set aside.

To assemble, fill the tart shell with the almond cream. Top with the roasted strawberries, extra tarragon and a generous sprinkling of candied almonds.

A cobbler sits somewhere deliciously in the middle of a pie and a crumble. The fruit base, made here with rhubarb and apple, is topped with sweet, scone-like biscuits, which are buttery and crisp. Apple and rhubarb is a classic combination, and the strawberries provide some extra juiciness – swap them out for raspberries or blackberries if you prefer. If you'd rather go the crumble route instead, my foolproof recipe is equal quantities of butter, flour, oats and half sugar. Just rub the butter into the dry ingredients with your fingertips until it resembles a crumble, then sprinkle it over the fruit and bake as below.

APPLE AND RHUBARB COBBLER

SERVES 4–6

500 g trimmed rhubarb stalks, cut into 1 cm lengths

3 granny smith apples (600 g), peeled, cored and cut into 3 mm thick slices

125 g strawberries, trimmed and large fruit halved

3 tablespoons raw sugar, plus extra for sprinkling

½ teaspoon finely ground fennel seeds

1 teaspoon vanilla extract

1 teaspoon plain flour

finely grated zest of 1 lemon

milk, for brushing

cream or vanilla ice cream, to serve

SOUR CREAM BISCUIT TOPPING

300 g (2 cups) plain flour, plus extra for dusting

100 g raw sugar

1 teaspoon baking powder

½ teaspoon ground cinnamon

pinch of fine sea salt

150 g chilled unsalted butter, cut into cubes

200 g sour cream

Preheat the oven to 180°C. Grease a deep 21 cm round baking dish with butter.

For the biscuit topping, combine the flour, sugar, baking powder, cinnamon and salt in the bowl of a food processor. Pulse a few times just to combine, then add the butter. Continue to pulse until you have a coarse sandy consistency. Add the sour cream and pulse until the mixture almost forms a ball. Tip the mixture onto a lightly floured work surface and gently bring the dough together using your hands. Flatten into a disc, cover and rest in the fridge for 15 minutes to firm up slightly.

Meanwhile, combine the fruit in a large bowl with the sugar, fennel, vanilla, flour and lemon zest. Toss to ensure everything is well coated. Pour into the baking dish.

On a lightly floured work surface, roll out the dough to a thickness of 4 mm. Using a 5 cm circle cutter, cut out rounds from the pastry and arrange them on top of the fruit. You can leave some space in between each biscuit as I have done, or overlap them a little for fuller biscuit coverage. Brush the rounds with milk and sprinkle with a little extra raw sugar. Bake for 40 minutes, or until the biscuits are golden and the fruit is bubbling.

Serve hot or warm with dollops of cream or vanilla ice cream.

Inspired by the Spanish shortbread *polvorones*, these fragrant buttery biscuits are simple to make and a delight to eat. I've suggested making them in a food processor for ease, but they can easily be mixed in a bowl, too. You will, however, still need to grind the nuts. While it's much easier to do this in a food processor, you can also use a mortar and pestle. Don't be tempted to substitute store-bought almond meal – the fine grind won't give you the desired results.

ROSE AND ALMOND BISCUITS

MAKES 24

125 g almonds

100 g icing sugar, plus extra for dusting

pinch of fine sea salt

250 g unsalted butter, softened

300 g (2 cups) plain flour, plus extra if needed

1 tablespoon rosewater

1 vanilla pod, split and seeds scraped, or 1 teaspoon vanilla bean paste

slivered pistachios, to garnish

rose petals, to garnish

Preheat the oven to 180°C. Line two baking trays with baking paper.

Place the almonds, icing sugar and salt in a food processor and blitz until the almonds are ground, but not too fine – about the texture of coarse sand. Add the butter and continue to blitz until the mixture is well combined. Add the flour, rosewater and vanilla and pulse until everything just comes together, scraping down the bowl with a spatula as you go if needed. The mixture should be soft but not sticky. Add more flour if necessary.

Roll the mixture into walnut-sized balls and arrange on the trays, allowing room for them to spread a little as they cook. Place the trays in the fridge for 10 minutes for the dough to firm up slightly.

Bake the biscuits for around 15 minutes until just beginning to colour around the edges – they will still be a little soft, but will firm up on cooling.

When cool enough to handle, but still warm, roll the biscuits in extra icing sugar, then allow to cool completely. Dust with extra icing sugar and top with pistachios and rose petals. The biscuits will keep in an airtight container for up to a week.

I love rhubarb in cakes. Not only does it look beautiful, even once cooked, but it adds a subtle sourness that counters the sweetness of baked treats. This cake is for my two friends Polly and Nova, whom I adore – they equally inspired me to create this cake and eventually write it down. They are both German, so this is affectionately known as German rhubarb cake in our home.

SPICED RHUBARB CRUMBLE CAKE

SERVES 8–10

150 g unsalted butter, softened

150 g raw sugar

2 eggs

1 vanilla pod, split and seeds scraped, or 1 teaspoon vanilla bean paste

finely grated zest of ½ lemon or orange

50 g (⅓ cup) almonds, coarsely ground (see Note page 184)

180 g (1¼ cups) plain flour

½ teaspoon baking powder

RHUBARB FILLING

350 g trimmed rhubarb stalks, cut into 1 cm pieces

2 tablespoons raw sugar

1 tablespoon plain flour

½ teaspoon ground ginger

generous pinch of freshly ground black pepper

2 cloves, ground

OAT TOPPING

210 g rolled oats

3 tablespoons raw sugar

1 tablespoon plain flour

generous pinch of sea salt

150 g chilled unsalted butter, cut into cubes, plus extra if needed

Preheat the oven to 180°C. Grease a 21 cm square cake tin with butter and line with baking paper.

Melt the butter in a small saucepan and simmer over a low heat for about 4 minutes until nutty and brown. Set aside to cool briefly.

In a large bowl, beat the sugar, eggs and vanilla until pale. Stir in the cooled butter, followed by the lemon or orange zest and the ground almonds. Sift in the flour and baking powder and mix until combined. Spoon the batter into the prepared tin and spread out evenly. Set aside.

For the filling, place the rhubarb in a bowl, sprinkle with the sugar, flour and spices and toss to coat. Scatter this mixture evenly into the cake tin, pressing the rhubarb gently into the batter.

To prepare the topping, mix the oats with the sugar, flour and salt and then add the butter. Toss to coat all the butter pieces and then, working quickly, use your fingertips to roughly rub the butter into the dry mixture until incorporated. You should be able to press the mixture together into large clumps. If it is too crumbly and not holding, add some extra butter.

Scatter the oat topping evenly over the rhubarb and and bake for 35–40 minutes until the top is golden and a skewer comes out clean when inserted in the centre of the cake.

Allow to cool slightly before serving.

CONVERSION CHARTS

Measuring cups and spoons may vary slightly from one country to another, but the difference is generally not enough to affect a recipe. All cup and spoon measures are level.

One Australian metric measuring cup holds 250 ml (8 fl oz), one Australian metric tablespoon holds 20 ml (4 teaspoons) and one Australian metric teaspoon holds 5 ml. North America, New Zealand and the UK use a 15 ml (3-teaspoon) tablespoon.

LIQUID MEASURES

One American pint = 500 ml (16 fl oz)
One Imperial pint = 600 ml (20 fl oz)

CUP	METRIC	IMPERIAL
⅛ cup	30 ml	1 fl oz
¼ cup	60 ml	2 fl oz
⅓ cup	80 ml	2½ fl oz
½ cup	125 ml	4 fl oz
⅔ cup	160 ml	5 fl oz
¾ cup	180 ml	6 fl oz
1 cup	250 ml	8 fl oz
2 cups	500 ml	16 fl oz
2¼ cups	560 ml	20 fl oz
4 cups	1 litre	32 fl oz

DRY MEASURES

The most accurate way to measure dry ingredients is to weigh them. However, if using a cup, add the ingredient loosely to the cup and level with a knife; don't compact the ingredient unless the recipe requests 'firmly packed'.

METRIC	IMPERIAL
15 g	½ oz
30 g	1 oz
60 g	2 oz
125 g	4 oz (¼ lb)
185 g	6 oz
250 g	8 oz (½ lb)
375 g	12 oz (¾ lb)
500 g	16 oz (1 lb)
1 kg	32 oz (2 lb)

LENGTH

METRIC	IMPERIAL
3 mm	⅛ inch
6 mm	¼ inch
1 cm	½ inch
2.5 cm	1 inch
5 cm	2 inches
18 cm	7 inches
20 cm	8 inches
23 cm	9 inches
25 cm	10 inches
30 cm	12 inches

OVEN TEMPERATURES

CELSIUS	FAHRENHEIT
100°C	200°F
120°C	250°F
150°C	300°F
160°C	325°F
180°C	350°F
200°C	400°F
220°C	425°F

CELSIUS	GAS MARK
110°C	¼
130°C	½
140°C	1
150°C	2
170°C	3
180°C	4
190°C	5
200°C	6
220°C	7
230°C	8
240°C	9
250°C	10

ACKNOWLEDGEMENTS

To my wonderful Plum family who show endless support, kindness and encouragement at every step of the book-making process. I feel incredibly lucky to have worked with you all again to create this beautiful book, which belongs to all of us. It is such a huge team effort and I couldn't do it without you all!

Mary Small, my visionary publisher. Thank you for believing in me all those years ago and putting your trust in me to go again! You also happen to be one of the loveliest humans, so thank you.

Clare Marshall, my project editor. Thank you for being such a dream to work with. I so appreciate all of your feedback and effortless ability to pull everything together! Thank you for all your encouragement throughout.

Thanks to Ash Carr – it was so great getting to know you and having you on the shoot. Thank you for all of your work behind the scenes.

Hannah Koelmeyer, thank you for your careful edits on what is a big task. It has been wonderful to be able to work with you again.

Armelle Habib, my treasured photographer who instantly makes me and everyone feel at ease. You have such an incredible talent and it always feels like we're making something very special when you're behind the lens. I'm honoured to be able to work with you on another book. Thank you for making it come to life with your images.

Karina Duncan, my absolutely amazing all-star stylist. You have such an effortless way about you and you always choose the right plate for the right dish every time. You totally get me and I couldn't dream of doing this with anybody else! I know a lot of effort goes into getting it right behind the scenes, and I so appreciate your attention to detail and the care that you put into sourcing and organising ceramics to be made specifically for the book. Thank you for making the food look so beautiful and for being a really great friend; so warm and wise. I can't wait to do it all again!

Michelle Mackintosh, my book designer and another woman with incredible vision. Thank you for your detailed eye and the tireless work that has gone into designing this book. I feel like I may be repeating myself, but like everyone else I have been fortunate enough to work with, you are simply an amazing human! You dream up things I can't even begin to imagine and I am so lucky to have you.

To the publicity team at Pan Macmillan, thank you for your hard work, support and encouragement.

To my kitchen crew: Sarah Watson, for stepping in on the cover day and taking the pressure off all of us in the kitchen. You are wonderful and I was so pleased you could be a part of this book; Allie King for also jumping in on the final week of shooting and being your bubbly, easygoing self, which brought a great spark to the set. You are amazing! Last, but by no means least, Emma Warren, who happens to be a fabulous author in her own right. Thank you for steering the kitchen ship so incredibly smoothly. So much goes into ensuring the shoot is as stress-free and breezy as possible and you do it all: scheduling, shopping, pep talks when something has gone awry, and without even blinking. I appreciate how much of yourself you bring to my books and I am immensely grateful for your support in the kitchen over the three-week shoot.

Thank you to Hannah Marshall for your hair and make-up expertise on set. You are amazing!

Grazie mille to Barbara Radice and Studio Sottsass in Milan for permission to use the lovely words of Ettore Sottsass in this book.

Thank you to all of the wonderful people who bought my first cookbook, *Ostro*. Seeing it in your kitchens and the food on your tables is incredibly humbling, and it is for all of you that I wrote it. Cooking is my greatest joy and to be able to share it with so many of you is truly a gift. I am thankful to be able to do it again and hope this book brings you good eating and lovely moments.

To every bookseller, journalist and fellow food writer who believed in me and *Ostro*, thank you for telling my story and recommending and supporting my work. This book wouldn't be possible without that support.

To all of my suppliers and food producers everywhere – butchers, bakers, fishmongers, cheesemongers, greengrocers and farmers, the list goes on. You inspire me to keep creating. The passion you show for your products is immeasurable. When something is so good, there isn't any need to complicate it. I so appreciate the early mornings, long hours and hard work that goes into producing our food.

To my friends and family. There are really too many of you to mention and you span many continents. Whether it be a simple phone call to check in or giving me feedback on a recipe, your support has not gone unnoticed.

Mum, thank you for always encouraging me in the kitchen, for buying me cookbooks as a teenager and for taking me to restaurants to try new foods. I am the cook I am today because of your nurturing, curiosity and enthusiasm. I still remember the stories you told me as a child of market adventures in Morocco and midnight feasts in Florence.

To my dear Nori, Haruki and Yukito, you really are my whole world and words cannot express how much love I have in my heart for you. Nori, you are my biggest cheerleader and your support never wavers. Thank you for staying up with me at 1 am when a cake has flopped for the third time. You are always willing to help clean up around me, workshop ideas and drive me to five different shops to find *that* ingredient. Haruki, this book is inspired by you, my love. The joy you bring to our little family is simply beyond, and sitting down together for a meal with you is my favourite part of the day. Thank you for helping to lick the bowl clean, peel the apples and sprinkle the salt. You are my sunshine! And to the newest member of our family, sweet little Yukito, I absolutely cannot wait to cook for you and with you.

A Plum book
First published in 2020 by
Pan Macmillan Australia Pty Limited
Level 25, 1 Market Street,
Sydney, NSW 2000, Australia

Level 3, 112 Wellington Parade,
East Melbourne, VIC 3002, Australia

Design by Michelle Mackintosh
Edited by Hannah Koelmeyer
Index by Helena Holmgren
Photography by Armelle Habib
Prop and food styling by Karina Duncan
Food preparation by Julia Busuttil Nishimura, Emma Warren and Sarah Watson
Typeset by Megan Ellis
Colour reproduction by Splitting Image Colour Studio
Printed and bound in China by 1010 Printing International Limited

A CIP catalogue record for this book is available from the National Library
of Australia.

Quote on page 10 © Ettore Sottsass / ADAGP, VISCOPY Paris, 2019

The publisher would like to thank Kate Brouwer of Asobimasu Clay for her
generosity in providing props for the book.

10 9 8 7 6 5 4 3